I0880371

UNDERSTANDING DAVE EGGERS

UNDERSTANDING CONTEMPORARY AMERICAN LITERATURE

Matthew J. Bruccoli, Founding Editor

Linda Wagner-Martin, Series Editor

Volumes on

Edward Albee | Sherman Alexie | Nelson Algren | Paul Auster
Nicholson Baker | John Barth | Donald Barthelme | The Beats
Thomas Berger | The Black Mountain Poets | Robert Bly | T. C. Boyle
Truman Capote | Raymond Carver | Michael Chabon | Fred Chappell
Chicano Literature | Contemporary American Drama
Contemporary American Horror Fiction
Contemporary American Literary Theory
Contemporary American Science Fiction, 1926–1970
Contemporary American Science Fiction, 1970–2000
Contemporary Chicana Literature | Robert Coover | Philip K. Dick
James Dickey | E. L. Doctorow | Rita Dove | Dave Eggers
John Gardner | George Garrett | Tim Gautreaux | John Hawkes | Joseph Heller
Lillian Hellman | Beth Henley | James Leo Herlihy | David Henry Hwang
John Irving | Randall Jarrell | Charles Johnson | Diane Johnson
Adrienne Kennedy | William Kennedy | Jack Kerouac | Jamaica Kincaid
Etheridge Knight | Tony Kushner | Ursula K. Le Guin | Denise Levertov
Bernard Malamud | David Mamet | Bobbie Ann Mason | Colum McCann
Cormac McCarthy | Jill McCorkle | Carson McCullers | W. S. Merwin
Arthur Miller | Stephen Millhauser | Lorrie Moore | Toni Morrison's Fiction
Vladimir Nabokov | Gloria Naylor | Joyce Carol Oates | Tim O'Brien
Flannery O'Connor | Cynthia Ozick | Suzan-Lori Parks | Walker Percy
Katherine Anne Porter | Richard Powers | Reynolds Price | Annie Proulx
Thomas Pynchon | Theodore Roethke | Philip Roth | Richard Russo | May Sarton
Hubert Selby, Jr. | Mary Lee Settle | Sam Shepard | Neil Simon
Isaac Bashevis Singer | Jane Smiley | Gary Snyder | William Stafford
Robert Stone | Anne Tyler | Gerald Vizenor | Kurt Vonnegut
David Foster Wallace | Robert Penn Warren | James Welch | Eudora Welty
Edmund White | Colson Whitehead | Tennessee Williams
August Wilson | Charles Wright

UNDERSTANDING

DAVE EGGERS

Timothy W. Galow

The University of South Carolina Press

© 2014 University of South Carolina

Published by the University of South Carolina Press
Columbia, South Carolina 29208

www.sc.edu/uscpress

Manufactured in the United States of America

23 22 21 20 19 18 17 16 15 14   10 9 8 7 6 5 4 3 2 1

Library of Congress Cataloging-in-Publication Data

Galow, Timothy W.
Understanding Dave Eggers / Timothy W. Galow.
pages cm. — (Understanding Contemporary American Literature)
Includes bibliographical references and index.
ISBN 978-1-61117-427-4 (hardback) — ISBN 978-1-61117-428-1 (ebook)
1. Eggers, Dave—Criticism and interpretation. I. Title.
PS3605.G48Z76 2014
813'.6—dc23

2014023116

This book was printed on recycled paper with 30 percent postconsumer waste content.

For Amy

CONTENTS

SERIES EDITOR'S PREFACE

The Understanding Contemporary American Literature series was founded by the estimable Matthew J. Bruccoli (1931–2008), who envisioned these volumes as guides or companions for students as well as good nonacademic readers, a legacy that will continue as new volumes are developed to fill in gaps among the nearly one hundred series volumes published to date and to embrace a host of new writers only now making their marks on our literature.

As Professor Bruccoli explained in his preface to the volumes he edited, because much influential contemporary literature makes special demands, "the word understanding in the titles was chosen deliberately. Many willing readers lack an adequate understanding of how contemporary literature works; that is, of what the author is attempting to express and the means by which it is conveyed." Aimed at fostering this understanding of good literature and good writers, the criticism and analysis in the series provide instruction in how to read certain contemporary writers—explicating their material, language, structures, themes, and perspectives—and facilitate a more profitable experience of the works under discussion.

In the twenty-first century Professor Bruccoli's prescience gives us an avenue to publish expert critiques of significant contemporary American writing. The series continues to map the literary landscape and to provide both instruction and enjoyment. Future volumes will seek to introduce new voices alongside canonized favorites, to chronicle the changing literature of our times, and to remain, as Professor Bruccoli conceived, contemporary in the best sense of the word.

Linda Wagner-Martin, Series Editor

CHAPTER 1

Understanding Dave Eggers

Dave Eggers rose to national prominence in 2000 with the publication of his first book, *A Heartbreaking Work of Staggering Genius.* The work, which the *Times* of London subsequently cited as one of the fifteen best books of the decade, quickly became a best seller and inspired a range of conversations about the author, postmodernism, and the state of literature in the twenty-first century.[1] Over the next decade, Eggers's works consistently climbed the best-seller lists and garnered nominations for both the National Book Critics Circle Award and the National Book Award. For his literary and extraliterary endeavors, he has also received honors as various as the Heinz Award for outstanding contributions to the Arts and Humanities (which comes with a $250,000 cash prize), the Dayton Literary Peace Prize, and the National Book Foundation's Literarian Award.

The film industry has helped to expand Eggers's renown, particularly in recent years. The film rights for Eggers's first two books were sold in 2002 and 2007, respectively, but the first film bearing his moniker did not appear until he wrote an original screenplay with his wife, Vendela Vida. *Away We Go,* a comedy about a couple looking for the ideal place to raise their first child, appeared in the summer of 2009, just a few months before Eggers's adaptation of Maurice Sendak's *Where the Wild Things Are* was released. More recently, Eggers's stories have been adapted for Gus Van Sant (*Promised Land,* 2012) and Jonathan Demme (*Zeitoun,* currently scheduled for a 2014 release).

Despite or perhaps in part because of Eggers's growing cultural prominence, his work has generated widely divergent responses in popular and critical circles. For some, Eggers's experimental bent and progressive activities make him a literary icon, a figure rightfully included in *The Outlaw Bible of American Literature.* A group of critics at the *Utne Reader,* to give just one example, named Eggers one of "50 Visionaries Who Are Changing the World."[2] Others see him as an ardent self-promoter whose public persona is a calculated façade. From this perspective, Eggers's string of awards and nominations is less a sign of some unique talent than it is a product of his popularity or, in a more extreme form of the argument, the literary establishment's insularity. The Underground Literary Alliance, a group of writers and critics who claim to be committed to exposing corruption in the publishing industry, had a brief (though periodically revisited) exchange with the author early in his career.[3]

Debates about Eggers's "true" commitments have only been exacerbated by his literary texts, which often interrogate the boundaries between fiction, memoir, and biography. Debates around his third major work, *What Is the What* (2006), have been particularly heated. In the book, Eggers retells the story of Valentino Achak Deng, a refugee from the Sudanese civil war that raged throughout the 1980s and early 1990s. The story, which emerged out of discussions between Deng and Eggers, is told in the first person. The work, however, is not just a mediated autobiography. Eggers freely admits inventing characters and events in the book, and he claims to have significantly altered the chronology for narrative effect. Some critics have found the postmodern underpinnings of the book a powerful way to convey horrors that might otherwise be incommunicable. The author Gary Krist has called the book "extraordinary" and claims that the unusual form yields "a document that—unlike so many 'real' autobiographies—exudes authenticity." It is worth noting that even in this positive review, Krist couches his praise in terms of Eggers's supposedly enormous ego: "the secret of the book's credibility lies in its author's success at excising his own oversized personality from the narrative."[4]

Many others have disagreed. Perhaps the most vociferous attack on *What Is the What* has come from the cultural critic Lee Seigel, who claims that the book's "innocent expropriation of another man's identity is a post-colonial arrogance."[5] To back up this charge, he says, "the eerie, slightly sickening quality about *What Is the What* is that Deng's personhood has been displaced by someone else's style and sensibility—by someone else's story. Deng survived his would-be killers in the Sudan, only to have his identity erased here."[6]

The tenor of these claims suggests something of the passion that Eggers has inspired in both his fans and his detractors. Debates about Eggers's personality, his literary politics, and his aesthetics have become so entrenched that even his first avowedly fictional book, *You Shall Know Our Velocity!*

(2002), is often read as a thinly veiled autobiography. The literary scholar Sarah Brouillette reads the novel "as a text about Eggers' career and his overriding concern with the idea of 'selling out.'" She concludes that the work "comes to exemplify one peculiar way in which Eggers' entire career is built circularly on reflections on itself, and the seeming impossibility of escaping such solipsism."[7]

With all the attention devoted to Eggers and his expanding literary concerns, a work specifically devoted to his texts is overdue. This is not to say that the current work attempts to address Eggers's books in an ahistorical vacuum. Instead, it focuses on those issues that have proved to be of greatest interest to contemporary readers, reviewers, and critics. Debates surrounding the texts have helped to shape the content of each chapter.

Beyond providing a degree of focus, these discussions are important because particular topics often become entrenched in public discussions. Scholars and critics examining Eggers's most recent texts, for instance, are often responding as much to previous works or debates about them as they are to the new text. When we place these books in relation to one another rather than, say, to the works of contemporaneous authors, it is possible to understand how such discussions have emerged and evolved.

Close attention to these texts also reveals which elements of Eggers's work carry over most directly from one text to the next and how Eggers's treatment of those elements changes over time. It would be possible, for instance, to read the strikingly sparse style of *Hologram for the King* (2012) as evidence of the author's ongoing concern with form. While such a broad generalization is certainly true, it neglects to account for the particular form of the text, and it ignores the larger movement in Eggers's work from the overblown self-awareness of *A Heartbreaking Work of Staggering Genius* to the pared-down prose of *Hologram.* Subsequent chapters could stand alone, each treating one particular text at some length, but they have been designed to show trends in Eggers's writing and to underscore major developments.

The following section surveys Eggers's professional career and briefly examines some of the nonliterary activities that inform his work, even though there is not enough space to pursue these links in the present volume. Many of Eggers's shorter texts and his nonliterary works, listed in the bibliography, are also neglected here for lack of space. As cofounder of the independent publishing firm McSweeney's and editor of several journals devoted to literature and film, Eggers has had his name put on hundreds of different texts and compilations in the past fifteen years. Beyond print, Eggers has dabbled in art, music, and film, producing or coproducing dozens of works. In order to provide a more substantial treatment of his major literary texts, a few of these efforts are treated rather summarily, and some are referred to only tangentially. Many, unfortunately, must be left out altogether.

Dave Eggers was born in Boston, Massachusetts, on March 12, 1970, the son of John K. Eggers (1936–1991) and Heidi McSweeney Eggers (1940–1992). Eggers was the third of four children, including Bill and Beth (three and two years his senior, respectively) and his younger brother, Christopher (thirteen years younger).

Eggers grew up in Lake Forest, Illinois, an affluent suburb of Chicago, and attended the University of Illinois at Champaign-Urbana, where he studied journalism and served as an editor at the *Daily Illini* ("Illini Union"). During his senior year, his father, an attorney, died unexpectedly from cancer. Several weeks later, Heidi, a schoolteacher, passed away after a struggle with stomach cancer. Suddenly parentless, the children relocated to California, where Beth was enrolled at law school. Over the next few years, Eggers commenced a promising career in publishing that drew on both his artistic talents and his journalism training. With an old friend from Chicago, David Moodie, Eggers took over a free newspaper and began work that developed into the satirical magazine *Might,* which ran from 1994 to 1997. The magazine gained national attention when it falsely announced the death of Adam Rich, a child star of the popular television show *Eight Is Enough.* The issue skewered media coverage of celebrity deaths, which Eggers has referred to as "customary . . . lionization, distortion, and exploitation."[8] The hoax, which Rich participated in, was quickly debunked, but not before word of his "death" had spread to his friends and acquaintances. The rise and fall of *Might,* as well as Eggers's personal struggles in the years after his parents' deaths, are loosely documented in his first major book, *A Heartbreaking Work of Staggering Genius.* The book begins with his mother's death and concludes with Eggers's decision to leave the San Francisco area shortly after the magazine folds.

By the time he left the Bay Area for the East Coast, Eggers had supplemented his work on *Might* with projects for Salon.com and *SF Weekly,* and he quickly found work in New York with *Esquire* and ESPN. In late 1998, Eggers turned his attention back to publishing and began *Timothy McSweeney's Quarterly Concern.* The first issue consisted entirely of stories that had been rejected by other magazines. While this conceit was dropped, *McSweeney's* quirky sensibility and imaginative content drew attention to the work of many talented young writers, some of whom had struggled to find an outlet for their writing. In an e-interview conducted shortly after the publication of *A Heartbreaking Work of Staggering Genius*, a representative from the Harvard *Advocate* worried that the periodical was no longer "publishing as many unknowns" and asked what steps might be taken to "keep shit real." The interview has remained in circulation primarily because of Eggers's scathing retort, which features a brief defense of the journal's vision and a lengthy rant about the idea of "selling out."[9]

McSweeney's established Eggers as a promising new figure in the literary world, but that position was, to put it mildly, confirmed in early 2000 with the publication of *A Heartbreaking Work of Staggering Genius*. The memoir became an immediate best seller and ran through nine print runs in its first months on the market. Vintage bid nearly $1.5 million for the rights to put out a paperback edition, and New Line Cinema put up nearly $2 million for movie rights.[10] Many critics were also quick with praise, and the work was named a Best Book of the Year by a number of major news outlets, including the *New York Times, Time,* and the *Washington Post*. The book was nominated for a Pulitzer Prize the following year, and Eggers received the Metcalfe Award, an annual prize for promising young artists, from the American Academy of Arts and Sciences.

Eggers generated even more publicity by going on a highly unconventional book tour. Many participants described the author's stops as fun and whimsical. Kim Curtis, a writer for the Associated Press, went to a reading at the City Lights bookstore in San Francisco where the audience wrote haikus about Condoleezza Rice, had their books decorated with glitter, and then took a bus to a bar in the Mission District with Eggers, who bought the crowd drinks.[11] The literary scholar Jonathan D'Amore described his own experience at a reading in Chapel Hill, North Carolina, in a very different way. Eggers, he claimed, showed up nearly thirty minutes late and "engaged in a long, transparent, and elaborately put on exchange with a man in the front row, who Eggers repeatedly claimed was David Foster Wallace. He would not read from *A Heartbreaking Work of Staggering Genius*." D'Amore, underscoring his own experience, also cited a reading in San Francisco that featured a local fire marshal speaking to the crowd for thirty minutes about fire safety.[12]

Eggers also used his newfound economic and cultural capital to promote McSweeney's, an outfit that now included the *Quarterly Concern,* a humorous website, and a publishing imprint. In its early years, McSweeney's put out books by such notable figures as David Byrne, Jonathan Lethem, Neal Pollack, and Lydia Davis. Eggers also began using the press for hardcover editions of his own books, beginning in 2002 with *You Shall Know Our Velocity*. (The exclamation point now commonly placed at the end of the title was added for the 2003 Vintage paperback edition.) For his efforts with McSweeney's and *You Shall Know Our Velocity!*, the Independent Publisher named Eggers Story-Teller of the Year.

In late 2002, Eggers teamed up with the educator Níneve Clements Calegari to cofound 826 Valencia, a volunteer tutoring center devoted to helping children "explore their creativity and improve their writing skills" (826 National). The name comes from the street address of the center. Local ordinances require that a portion of the space be devoted to retail activities, so the front of the building serves as a pirate supply store, selling peg legs, cutlasses, and lard.[13] The program has since developed into 826 National, with independently operated sister centers in Boston, Chicago, New York City, Washington, D.C., Seattle, Ann Arbor, and Los Angeles. The whimsical storefront has traveled with the program. The 826 in Boston, for instance, is fronted by the Greater Boston Bigfoot Research Institution, and the center in Brooklyn outfits superheroes. Eggers also drew on the recommendations of students for the first volume of *The Best American Nonrequired Reading* (2002). The series has continued through the present with introductions provided by people as various as Zadie Smith, Beck, and Guillermo del Toro. Cover art has been contributed by notable figures such as Art Spiegelman, Banksy, and Maurice Sendak.

After the release of *You Shall Know Our Velocity!* in 2002, Eggers published a number of smaller works in 2003, including a collection of short stories under the pseudonym Lucy Thomas (*Jokes Told in Heaven about Babies*) and a fake science manual written with Toph under the names Dr. and Mr. Doris Haggis-On-Whey (*Giraffes? Giraffes!*). More notably, he published a revised and slightly expanded version of *You Shall Know Our Velocity!* under the title *Sacrament* and began a new journal, *The Believer*, under the McSweeney's umbrella. Originally planned as *The Optimist*, *The Believer* asserts in its mission statement that it is devoted to "writers and books [the editors] like" and will "give people and books the benefit of the doubt" ("About the *Believer*"). Vendela Vida, whom Eggers married in 2003, still serves as an editor for the journal.

In 2004, Eggers started another notable philanthropic venture with Dr. Lola Vollen, a visiting scholar at the University of California at Berkeley with a distinguished record of human rights activism. Eggers and Vollen met while he was teaching at the Graduate School of Journalism, and together they founded Voice of Witness, a nonprofit organization devoted to publishing the stories of people affected by human rights abuses. To date, the organization has put out a dozen books, two of which were tied directly to Eggers's next major literary works, *What Is the What* (2006) and *Zeitoun* (2009).

Also in 2004, McSweeney's introduced *Wholphin,* a DVD magazine featuring "short films, documentaries, instructional videos, foreign sitcoms, and other cinema hybrids" ("About"). Eggers put out another "science" book with Toph (*Your Disgusting Head*), edited several collections (*The Future Dictionary of America* and *Created in Darkness by Troubled Americans: The Best of McSweeney's Humor Category*), cowrote, with Níneve Clements Calegari and Daniel Moulthrop, a book about the current state of teaching (*Teachers Have It Easy: The Big Sacrifices and Small Salaries of America's Teachers*), and serialized a story on Salon.com, which McSweeney's later printed under the title *The Unforbidden Is Compulsory, or Optimism.*

As if this were not enough for one year, Eggers published his first collection of short stories, *How We Are Hungry* in 2004, and Penguin released a collection of Eggers's microfiction, *Short Short Stories,* in 2005. (*Hungry* was a finalist for an Independent Publishing Award, and *The Future Dictionary* won in the humor category.) Nothing Eggers published in the years immediately after *A Heartbreaking Work of Staggering Genius* received the same degree of critical or popular support as his first book, but the continued success of McSweeney's and Eggers's expanding philanthropic activities garnered much attention. In 2005, he was named one of *Time*'s 100 Most Influential people, and Brown University gave him an honorary doctorate.

During this whirlwind period, Eggers continued to work on his next major project, a collaboration with the Sudanese "Lost Boy" Valentino Achak Deng. Their relationship was close enough that the book, *What Is the What* (2006), is called both an "Autobiography" and "A Novel by Dave Eggers" on the title page. The story, which documents both Deng's immense hardships during the Second Sudanese Civil War and his struggles after being relocated to Atlanta, reflects Eggers's increased engagement with issues of social justice and his penchant for humanitarian projects. The proceeds from the book go to the newly founded Valentino Achak Deng Foundation, a nonprofit organization that supports Deng's schooling in the United States and provides ongoing support for people affected by the conflict in Sudan. In May 2009, the Foundation opened a secondary school in Marial Bai, Deng's hometown in southern Sudan. This collaboration was also followed by a Voice of Witness text, *Out of Exile: The Abducted and Displaced People of Sudan.*

What proved to be another major best seller and garnered rave reviews from many critics, who praised both its artistry and its pathos. It was nominated for a National Critics Book Circle Award the following year and won the Prix Médicis étranger, an annual French literary prize, in 2009. In recent years, the text has been distributed as required reading to freshman at a number of major universities, including Duke, the University of Maryland, and the University of Maine. The success of *What* was compounded by publicity for numerous other prizes Eggers received during this period, including a TED Prize for his educational endeavors and a $250,000 Heinz Award for extraordinary achievement in the arts and humanities.

After *What,* Eggers published a second collection of short short stories, *How Water Feels to the Fishes,* as part of a box set entitled *One Hundred and Forty-Five Stories in a Small Box.* The box set also included Sarah Manguso's *Hard to Admit and Harder to Escape* and Deb Olin Unferth's *Minor Robberies.* The collection was reviewed positively but was overshadowed by the continued success of *What* and of Eggers's next book-length project, *Zeitoun* (2009). The work, like its predecessor, emerged out of a lengthy interview process. This time Eggers worked with the Zeitoun family, whose story had been included in the Voice of Witness text *Voices from the Storm: The People of New Orleans on Hurricane Katrina and Its Aftermath.* The book, listed unequivocally as nonfiction, recounts the Zeitoun family's harrowing experiences during and after Hurricane Katrina, when Abdulrahman, the patriarch, was arrested by officials from the U.S. Department of Homeland Security. Again, the book became a best seller and received a number of accolades, including the Dayton Literary Peace Prize. Eggers was also awarded the Courage in Media award by the Council on American-Islamic Relations and the *Los Angeles Times* Innovators Award for his "multifaceted, spirited commitment to literature."[14] As with *What,* the proceeds from the book went to a nonprofit foundation.

The year 2009 also marked Eggers's Hollywood debut, with the release of *Away We Go,* a Sam Mendes film for which Eggers and Vida had written the script, and *Where the Wild Things Are,* directed by Spike Jonze. For the latter project, Eggers adapted Maurice Sendak's esteemed children's story into both a feature-length film and a novel that was released in conjunction with the film's premiere. Of the three projects, Jonze's film received the most attention, as well as a few award nominations, though none of the endeavors proved to be major successes. In terms of Eggers's popular reception, this cluster of works did serve as a reminder of the author's diverse ambitions, which, by 2009, could easily have been overshadowed by his philanthropic projects and his widely praised nonfiction texts. They also mark an interesting turn toward issues of parenting and childhood, not a surprising shift after the birth of October Adelaide Eggers Vida in late 2005.

Eggers continued to diversify his output the following year with a book of drawings, *It Is Right to Draw Their Fur* (2010), which was put out in conjunction with his first solo art show, at Electric Works in San Francisco. Back in 2008, Eggers had curated a collection at apexart in New York and, at the same time, put out an issue of the *Quarterly Concern* (#27) that interrogated the formal boundaries of art. In the issue, Eggers raised questions both about the way drawings are categorized (sketches, doodles, finished works) and about the relationship between drawings and text. *It Is Right* picks up on these concerns with a series of "sketches" that defy easy categorization. Many of the works are rough drawings of animals paired with eccentric captions.

In recent years, Eggers has grabbed fewer headlines with major new initiatives, but this seems to be less a sign of decreased activity than it is a reflection of the author's ongoing commitments. From philanthropic activities to family obligations to publishing concerns, Eggers continues to juggle and to remain productive in an impressive array of endeavors. His most recent literary project, *A Hologram for the King* (2012), was both a best seller and a finalist for the National Book Award. Surprising as it might seem after Eggers's fifteen years of literary activity, *Hologram* could be considered only the second novel Eggers has written. (In summations of the author's work, particularly those at the beginning of his books, *What Is the What* is generally categorized as fiction. The story, however, is deeply invested in Valentino Achak Deng's life and experiences, making such a simple demarcation somewhat problematic.)

In terms of Eggers's larger oeuvre, *Hologram* is an unusual work that can be viewed simultaneously as a return, a continuation, and a departure. The narrative, which focuses on a morose American searching for meaning in a foreign country, revisits ground covered in some of Eggers's early stories. (It bears more than a passing resemblance to his first novel, *You Shall Know Our Velocity!*). At the same time, *Hologram* draws heavily on the thematic concerns of his more recent works and continues, albeit in a slightly different form, previous meditations on the human costs of economic and political developments around the globe. The middle-aged protagonist also brings a perspective that is quite different from that of Eggers's earlier and much younger American leads.

The remainder of this book traces a number of discontinuities and developments through Eggers's literary works. Most chapters focus specifically on one text, but analyses implicitly and explicitly position each text in relation to others. Similarly, the discussions situate Eggers's work within critical conversations about his texts and about contemporary literature more generally. In order to maintain focus on a given work, however, the details of these debates are often briefly summarized or elided. References to important scholarly analyses can be found throughout, and full citations are available at the end of the book.

CHAPTER 2

A Heartbreaking Work of Staggering Genius

Dave Eggers's first book, *A Heartbreaking Work of Staggering Genius* (2000),[1] was preceded by a wave of advance publicity and literary buzz, including an early excerpt in *The New Yorker* and a laudatory article in *Time* just prior to the book's release. When the work finally appeared, it quickly climbed best-seller lists around the country and ignited discussions in a range of magazines and journals.[2]

On its most basic level, Eggers's book, which he describes in the acknowledgments as a "memoir-y kind of thing" (xxii), details what happened to him over several years following the deaths of his parents. Both died of cancer within weeks of each other, leaving Eggers, at age twenty-one, the primary caretaker for his eight-year old brother, Christopher. Eggers and Toph, as he is addressed throughout the text, go to California with their older sister, Beth, who will be attending law school at Berkeley. Their older brother, Bill, also relocates to L.A., though he appears infrequently throughout the text. They spend the summer with Beth's friend Katie and Eggers's girlfriend, Kirsten, at a house in San Francisco, where he hopes to "re-create domestic life, from scratch, without precedent" (61). The remainder of the book documents Eggers's efforts to come to terms with his losses and the difficulties of beginning postcollegiate life in a new part of the country with a dependent child in tow.

Many critics have praised the work for its blend of "genuine, unsentimental poignancy"[3] and "merciless" self-critical humor.[4] Yet commentary has tended to focus on the text's intense self-consciousness and, in particular, the challenges that this self-consciousness raises for a "realistic" memoir. The work begins with more than forty pages of prefatory material, including a copyright page littered with authorial interjections and six "Rules and

Suggestions for Enjoyment of this Book." (Eggers deems much of his work "uneven" and advises the reader to skip large sections of the text.) A brief preface documents some of the ways in which characters, dialogue, and settings have been "fictionalized." It also reproduces a series of passages and epigraphs that were omitted from the main body of the text. The opening materials conclude with a lengthy acknowledgments section that contains a list of major themes from the book, an incomplete guide to symbols and metaphors, an account of the initial payment Eggers received for writing the book, and a hand-drawn picture of a stapler. The first Vintage paperback edition, published in early 2001, also includes an appendix, "Mistakes We Knew We Were Making," that was printed upside-down and in reverse at the back of the book, thereby turning the end of the text into another beginning. This addendum contains more "corrections, notations, updates, tangential remarks and clarifications" that provide information about the construction and reception of the text.

As this brief summation suggests and as numerous critics have pointed out, these "paratexts" challenge the conventions of memoir writing and scrutinize the genre's implicit claims to truth.[5] In the opening pages of the text, Eggers replaces the standard disclaimer about fictionalization with the claim that "all characters and incidents and dialogue are real, are not products of the author's imagination, because at the time of this writing, the author had no imagination whatsoever for those sorts of things, and could not conceive of *making up* a story or characters—it felt like driving a car in a clown suit" (iv). He then opens the preface by conceding that, despite "all the author's bluster elsewhere, this is not, actually a work of pure nonfiction." This admission precedes a lengthy accounting, which runs throughout the paratextual materials, of the many ways in which the narrative deviates from reality. He even claims, at the beginning of "Mistakes," that the primary purpose of this "corrective appendix" is to "illuminate the many factual and temporal fudgings necessary to keep this, or really any, work of nonfiction, from dragging around in arcane and endless explanations of who was exactly where, and when" (5). If these accounts underscore the fictionality of Eggers's memoir, they also reveal an impulse to rehabilitate, at least partially, the book's reliability by exposing its "scaffolding."

In one of the textual "omissions" included in the preface, the narrator admits, "I like the scaffolding. I like the scaffolding as much as I like the building. Especially if the scaffolding is beautiful, in its way" (xii). While this seems like a fairly straightforward assertion, the location of the remark calls its validity into question. First, the statement has been officially designated as an omission, suggesting that it should be disregarded. At the same time, the passage is still included in the book. Second, it is not entirely clear where this passage originated. It could have been part of an earlier draft of the book, but it is also possible that it was created for the "Omissions" section. Third, even if the passage was removed from the main body of the text, it is not clear why. Did Eggers remove it for philosophical reasons? Aesthetic? A momentary whim during the revision process? These questions suggest the playful and, for some, infuriating nature of Eggers's prefatory materials.

Eggers continues to highlight the process of construction within the narrative itself. He repeatedly mentions staying up late at night to write and occasionally mentions carrying a notebook or a tape recorder to capture his immediate impressions of events for use in the memoir. In interviews, Eggers has repeatedly justified this approach with appeals to a larger sense of truth: "to ignore the notebook, to pretend like it wasn't there—that's not entirely honest. And the goal was to make [the book] painfully honest."[6] From this perspective, the text's undercurrent of self-consciousness does not merely intrude on a closed narrative world but is itself a crucial element of that world. Eggers is not simply writing about the loss of his parents and all the changes that their loss entailed. He is writing a story about writing the story of that loss. "Self-awareness is sincerity," he asserts in "Mistakes" (34).

Accordingly, most events in the text are accompanied by an undercurrent of self-doubt, a constant questioning of motivation. When Eggers arrives at Lake Michigan late at night to dispose of his mother's ashes, he notes, "look what I'm doing, with my tape recorder and notebook, and here at the beach, with this box-calculating, manipulative, cold, exploitive." When he finally throws her remains in the lake, he comments, "I am doing something both beautiful but gruesome because I am destroying its beauty by knowing that it might be beautiful" (395).

The narrator's powerful self-consciousness also helps to shape the form of the book. Many chapters are constructed around simple, linear events. The main action of the opening chapter revolves around Dave and his sister, Beth, trying to stop their mother's nosebleed. In the late stages of stomach cancer, Heidi's blood will not clot properly, but she resists going to the hospital. After several hours, they finally convince her to go, and the chapter ends with the family lying on cots in her hospital room. Around this relatively simple story, the forty-four-page chapter moves quickly from childhood scenes to details of his mother's deterioration and his father's recent passing. It even includes a manic flash-forward that outlines the events after Heidi's death, which is not directly depicted in the chapter. All of these accounts are interspersed with Eggers's own self-conscious reflections and imaginative interjections, some of which expand into distinct vignettes that punctuate the larger scenes. Eggers, for instance, spends a half page imagining his mom's cancer as a cluster of tiny cities with "unruly, sprawling, environmentally careless citizenry" (4).

Many of the subsequent chapters follow a similar structure. Chapter 2 details a drive to the beach in San Francisco, a relatively short trip that takes twenty-five pages. This form documents the steady progression of present events as they are reflected through a scattered mind, one that is motivated by both conscious and unconscious forces. Again, Eggers's text does not simply aim to recount moments from his life or detail his psychological responses to them. The text itself is positioned as part of his ongoing response to his parents' deaths.

If Eggers's associative links, imaginative leaps, and rambling self-consciousness help to shape the narrative, they also occasionally disrupt the story, as when Toph interrupts the flow of narration to criticize the artificial compression of events: "it was almost as if it was too much to happen in one day, as if a number of days had been spliced together to quickly paint a picture of an entire period of time . . . without having to stoop (or rise) to actually pacing the story out" (114). On one level, this kind of interjection reinforces Eggers's desire to capture the truth behind the artifice of writing. This story did not emerge wholly formed, as a reflection of some factual experience. Its creation entailed much revision (part of the reason for including "omitted" passages in the preface) and self-doubt. Some of this conflict is captured in the ensuing conversation with Toph, which examines Eggers's motives for writing the book and recasts earlier events. In the opening chapter, for instance, their father, John, is depicted as a headstrong man full of "minor miracles." During the profound moment of self-doubt represented by his conversation with Toph, however, Eggers begins to revise this account. He refers to their "semi-violent alcoholic household" and mentions his father's failed time in Alcoholics Anonymous. This new narrative unfolds slowly, a reflection of Eggers's psychological struggle with the difficult material, and culminates at the end of the book with an anecdote about his father breaking down the door of his bedroom in a rage.

The roundabout narrative style as a whole operates in a similar way. It circles around the most painful elements of Eggers's past as he slowly processes the traumatic events and attempts to start a new life in California. If the form of the work supports the author's contention that the book aims to be "painfully honest," Eggers, in this particular conversation with Toph, provides a more nuanced account of the book's "realism." Toph argues that the story feels artificial. It manipulates reality to elicit a response from readers, not to construct a truthful account of events. In the ensuing argument, Eggers concedes that literal transcription is impossible: "to adequately relate even five minutes of internal thought-making would take forever." He then acknowledges the formal limitations of narrative writing. "This story," he says, "is just a caricature, this, the skeleton of experience" that ultimately provides only "one, two dimensions of twenty" (115). In short, writing about real events always involves choosing pertinent details to discuss and organizing them in a coherent manner, processes that transform "reality" into a focused and engaging narrative.

Eggers presses this point further in other self-conscious asides by suggesting that language is itself inadequate to capture "real" life. Eggers returns, for instance, to an explicit discussion of the text after another difficult event, when one of his friends swallows a handful of pills and is rushed to the hospital. The narrator muses, "I could be aware of the dangers of the self-consciousness, but at the same time, I'll be plowing through . . . mixed metaphors, noise, and will try to show the core, which is still there, as a core, and is valid, despite the fog. . . . There is always the core, that can't be articulated" (270). The inadequacy of language is further underscored when Eggers's friend tries to coax him into giving an inspirational speech. Though he finally concedes and consoles his friend, the speech is not transcribed in the book. Instead, Eggers dismissively notes that he is "piecing [it] together from times I've seen it done on TV and in the movies." He concludes, "I make myself sick saying it all, everything so obvious, the reasons to live not at all explainable in a few minutes on the edge of a psychiatric ward bed, but still he is roused, making me wonder even more about him" (279).

These responses are consistent with Eggers's desire to express a form of truth in his memoir, even if a simple or literal transcription of reality is never possible. His friend exemplifies the unsophisticated media consumer who is looking for an easy emotional payoff, one that can be provided by formulaic speeches and stock scenarios. By extension, *A Heartbreaking Work of Staggering Genius* positions itself as a probing, self-aware text that transcends such trivial expressions and indirectly expresses "the core."

This interpretation succinctly captures one facet of the book, a side emphasized by critics who would dismiss Eggers as a condescending hipster. However, to highlight only this one aspect of the text is to miss another, equally important dimension. Eggers repeatedly underscores the inadequacy of his own perspective in a variety of ways. During the previous exchange, Eggers's suicidal friend complains about the way he is being characterized in the book. He even threatens to walk out of the narrative after a heated exchange. In addition, the narrator, as he does throughout the text, punctuates his criticisms of others with comments that demonstrate his own inadequacies. After ranting for an entire page about wasted potential and useless self-pity, Eggers concludes the chapter by admitting that he has, during his tirade, become literally lost. His car is nowhere to be seen.

The opening of the next chapter continues to undercut Eggers's position by implicitly aligning him with the friend that he has just vehemently criticized. When first entering his friend's room, Eggers learns that another patient defecated all over the floor the previous night. The subsequent chapter opens with a discussion of a toilet overflow that has left excrement all over Eggers's office floor (283).

The seemingly contradictory perspectives joined in the text also complicate the larger message that certain passages seem to convey, namely that *A Heartbreaking Work of Staggering Genius* strives to transcend banality and get at "the core." If, as Eggers suggests, "the core" itself cannot be directly articulated, readers are forced to infer the true meaning from the text, a text that always inadequately reconstructs past events. To complicate matters further, the text repeatedly foregrounds the limitations of individual perspectives. Eggers, even in his most confident and self-assured moments, is constantly being challenged by others' versions of events and visions of the world. Late in the book, Eggers returns to Chicago for a friend's wedding and has sex with a girl that he has idealized since childhood. He wakes in the morning with a powerful feeling of connection and renewal, as if "some sort of bridge that was in disarray . . . is now rebuilt, redesigned, and new, pristine, wonderful" (393). Even as Eggers is planning to spend the morning with Sarah, he finds himself suddenly alone on the street in front of her apartment, ejected after a few hasty comments and vague excuses.

Such rapid deflations and reversals occur throughout the text and often force the narrator to admit his own confusion, not just about the attitudes of others but also about his own motivations. At some point in their hasty parting, Sarah makes a remark about "getting what he wanted," a comment that, for the narrator, seems to have come out of nowhere. As he attempts to "make the words work, to make them sound familiar, have them make sense," he realizes that he cannot articulate what it was that he hoped to gain from this encounter (393). "It is all hazy," he admits in a defeated tone that strongly contrasts with the moments of bravura scattered throughout the text. If at points Eggers positions himself as a bold purveyor of a new brand of literary consciousness and a fierce critic of conventional attitudes, at other moments he seems more like a bystander to his own life, recording thoughts and events that he seems largely unable to explain.

From the latter perspective, the details he reveals about his life do not point to some larger truth, any more than, to use Eggers's metaphor, an abandoned snakeskin might reveal some profound information about its former owner. He asks, "Do we know where the snake is now? No. By now the snake could be wearing fur; the snake could be selling pencils in Hanoi. The skin is no longer his." These discarded fragments can certainly be interpreted by readers, but their interpretations tell us nothing of value about the snake beyond "this approximate girth and that approximate length" (216). In fact, these stories/skins only complicate matters by producing more versions of a particular being. They do not pin down or reduce a figure to a singular interpretation. Instead, Eggers claims, "it's just the opposite, more is more is more" (215).

Again, taken to the extreme, this picture of proliferating skins and interpretations suggests that *A Heartbreaking Work of Staggering Genius* is not so much a statement of truth as one partial vision of a particular series of events, a flash of rhetorical theater that documents little more than its own production. Accordingly, Eggers often foregrounds his own narrative artifice and underscores the constructed nature of the text. The second chapter, for instance, begins under the open California sky, a striking contrast to the dark, insular rooms that dominate the first chapter. This shift reflects the children's newfound sense of freedom, which results from both the initial influx of insurance money and the sudden lack of parental oversight. The expansiveness of this new world is emphasized in a cinematic opening that positions the reader high above the car as it speeds along the highway: "Please look. Can you see us? Can you see us, in our little red car? Picture us from above, as if you were flying above us, in say, a helicopter, or on the back of a bird, as our car hurtles . . . around the relentless, sometimes ridiculous bends of Highway 1" (47). By directly addressing the reader, Eggers emphasizes the way in which an (explicitly visual) perspective is being constructed through the narrative. Moreover, the passage reminds readers that they are not witnessing a life but viewing that which has been consciously and deliberately put on display.

Such formulations, present in various forms throughout the text, threaten to blur, if not altogether erase, the line between fiction and reality. Eggers plays with the distinction even more explicitly in his acknowledgments section. For anyone who might deem a "memoir-y kind of thing" to be of low literary merit, he offers a very simple piece of advice: "PRETEND IT'S FICTION" (xxiv). For those who would reject the claim that fiction and nonfiction are distinguished only in the mind of the reader, Eggers offers another solution. He will send readers an electronic copy of the book so that they can insert new names into the text. "*Voila!*" he concludes (xxiv). "Fiction!"

While these suggestions playfully engage the reader, at other points in the text Eggers addresses his audience in a more aggressive manner. When the narrator dismisses his text as a dead snakeskin, he attacks people for their desire to uncover "the truth" and imagines the reader as "a panhandler, begging for anything" (215). This description makes the audience sound a lot like Eggers's much-maligned suicidal friend, who could care less where the words come from so long as they provide a sufficient emotional charge. The reader of memoirs, in this interpretation, is simply out for the vicarious thrill proffered by others' "real" experiences.

In other moods, Eggers envisions these same readers as potential members of his "lattice," a collection of interconnected souls who support one another and, through their relationships, make the whole group stronger (211). In some instances, as in the book's concluding rant, the impulses to dismiss and to embrace the audience merge in a stream of alternating attacks and entreaties: "Don't you know that I am connected to you? Don't you know that I'm trying to pump blood to you, that this is for you, that I hate you people, so many of you motherfuckers—When you sleep I want you never to wake up . . . when you're all sleeping so many sleeping I am somewhere on some stupid rickety scaffolding and I'm trying to get your stupid fucking attention I've been trying to show you this, just been trying to show you this" (437).

These comments close the text with a striking reminder of the ambivalences that have run throughout the narrative. Eggers has explicitly attempted to create a "painfully honest" account of his own life, an account that perhaps can cut through "the fog" to reveal an ill-defined "core." Yet his efforts are constrained by the limitations of language and literary history, by the dynamics of reading and the psychology of readers, and by his own personal limitations. His efforts are so constrained that, at points, he seems willing to concede that his work is little more than an elaborate fiction, a grand illusion that bears as much resemblance to a formulaic sitcom as it does to his "real" life.

Many commentators have noted Eggers's apparent unwillingness to mediate, synthesize, or otherwise come to terms with the oppositional views that run throughout the text. Instead, his mood vacillates between extremes in what the *New York Times* critic Michiko Kakutani has called a "manic-depressive stew of a book," a comment that is, not incidentally, included on the cover of paperback editions of the text.[7] *A Heartbreaking Work of Staggering Genius* is a book that foregrounds its own bipolarity, trumping up its theatricality even as it champions painful honesty. In the process, the terms at play quickly become unstable and defy easy categorization. The narrator, for instance, highlights the discrepancies between language and reality, suggesting that his book is always a form of fiction. This admission, however, suggests that his avowedly inadequate story actually reflects the impossible struggle to capture truth on the page.

Such binaries litter the text, as major elements are constantly being thrown against their opposites in a way that simultaneously suggests ineradicable tension and mutual dependence. In his elaborate list of the book's themes, Eggers suggests that literary self-consciousness can quickly become conventional and, hence, not really be self-conscious at all: "[Theme] C) The Painfully, Endlessly Self-Conscious Book Aspect . . . / C.2) The Knowingness about the Book's Self-Consciousness Aspect / While the author is self-conscious about being self-referential, he is also knowing about the self-conscious self-referentiality . . . he also plans to be clearly, obviously aware of his knowingness about his self-consciousness of self-referentiality" (xxix–xxx). At another point in the list, he considers the way in which his self-deprecation in the book can easily be seen from a different perspective as a form of self-promotion: "P) The Self-Aggrandizement as Art Form Aspect / Q) The Self-Flagellation as Art Form Aspect / R) The Self-Aggrandizement Disguised as Self-Flagellation as Even Higher Art Form Aspect / S) The Self-Canonization Disguised as Self-Destruction Masquerading as Self-Aggrandizement Disguised as Self-Flagellation as Highest Art Form of All Aspect" (xxxvii).

Such oppositions also emerge, though often a bit more subtly, throughout the main body of the text. During the opening chapters, for instance, Eggers asserts his desire to create a "new model" of family. For a brief period, he and Toph live with their sister, Beth, her friend Katie, and Dave's girlfriend, Kirsten. The narrator imagines it as an ideal household, "like a commune! Sharing the babysitting, the cleaning, the cooking! Big meals together, parties, joy!" Within a couple of days, the "family" quickly degenerates into petty squabbles, with the "resulting skirmishes making the place claustrophobic" (62). After he and Toph wind up in their own place, Eggers maintains his hope that they will represent a viable new form of family, even as the story underscores the ways in which their actions sometimes reinforce conventional attitudes and behaviors. Finally, during their narrative-disrupting conversation, Toph confronts his brother: "so far you've been very priggish and controlling, and for all your bluster you end up maintaining most of their customs, the rules imposed by our parents. Especially the secrecy. For instance, you hardly ever let my friends come over, because you don't want them to see how messy the house is, how we live" (116). Despite Eggers's genuine desire to create something new, he repeatedly underscores how something that seems novel can actually reinforce aspects of the status quo.

The subject comes up again when Eggers and a friend have a shared fantasy about a life without constraints. In this life, they imagine, "we wake up, tear the world down to its foundations, or below that even, and then, by three in the afternoon, we've got a new world . . . every day we create everything from scratch" (145). The desire for unrestrained freedom appears in many forms throughout the text, and, in his more optimistic moments, the narrator champions the power of creativity. Indeed, the book as a whole could be seen as Eggers's attempt to transcend the traditional constraints of autobiography and to create a new kind of memoir. This desire for innovation, however, can never entirely escape the bounds of history. This book, for all of its emphasis on creation and innovation, is itself a testament to Eggers's struggles with the past and the ongoing, though always changing, influence of his parents. Similarly, if Eggers's text as a whole stands as a testament to his desire for innovation, its innovations make sense only in the context of a larger Western tradition of letters. As Eggers ponders writing a story about his friend's attempted suicide, the narrator's primary concern is finding a way to do something different: "People have done stuff about suicides before. But I could twist it somehow, include random things. . . . That's a good detail, the laughing while your friend is having his stomach pumped. People have done that, too. Probably on TV even, *Picket Fences* maybe. But I could take it further. . . . I could be aware, for instance, in the text, of it having been done before, but that I have no choice but to do it again. . . . But then it will sound like one of those things where the narrator, having grown up media-saturated, can't live through anything without it having echoes of similar experiences in television. . . . So I'll have to take it past that" (269).

Beyond the challenge of actually creating something new, Eggers struggles with the speed at which things that might initially seem novel can become commonplace or boring. The text as a whole moves through a series of such shifts. The second chapter depicts Eggers's attempts to establish new living arrangements in California. Over the next several chapters, the novelty of their situation is replaced by oppressive routine and the mundane difficulties of life as a working single parent. In sections V and VI, Eggers seems reinvigorated by his efforts to create *Might* magazine, but, after the first flush of excitement, the work quickly becomes routine. The book concludes with a section that parallels the drive to the beach in part 2, only this time the sense of exuberant freedom is replaced by a feeling of confinement: "San Francisco was getting small, and everyone is dying. The summers are getting colder, and the falls aren't what they used to be. . . . And the drive to work was getting unbearable, the repetition too sad, especially at night, when after putting Toph to bed, locking the door, I would go back to the office—the drive just harrowing, the routine" (411). The book closes with Eggers and Toph prepared to leave, to go anywhere that promises a fresh start.

All of the binary terms touched on here are significant in the text (creation and conformity, the promise of the future and dependence on the past, self-deprecation and self-aggrandizement, critical and rote self-consciousness, truth and falsity, sincerity and manipulative posturing, theatricality and direct representation, the reader as comrade and as antagonist). Long as this list has already gotten, it touches on only a small number of oppositions that collide and transform throughout the text. The slipperiness of the work is further exacerbated by the narrator's voice, which the writer and cultural critic Lee Siegel has referred to as "post-postmodern half-irony—call it sincerony."[8] Siegel, in his explanation of this definition, turns to Eggers's title, which seems to mock artistic ambition while also leaving open the possibility that, as Eggers himself puts it in his acknowledgments, "the author is dead serious in his feeling that the title is an accurate description of the content, intent, and quality of the book" (xxvi). Similarly, the title foregrounds the emotional struggle at the center of the book while also seeming to undercut some aspect of that very struggle or its representation.

While Siegel objects to this blend of literary gamesmanship and personal pain, his analysis of the title looks very much like Eggers's own. The primary difference is that Siegel, as one might expect from a cultural critic, resolves the tension by explaining what he takes to be Eggers's real and final aim, allowing "modest, self-mocking decency [to] be celebrated as a kind of art."[9] In contrast, Eggers spends the better part of a page musing over the title's potential slipperiness before he simply dismisses the issue: "does it even matter now? Hells no. You're here, you're in, we're havin' a party!"

It is precisely the author's unwillingness to settle his terms, as Siegel adeptly notes, that makes the book so difficult to characterize. The author's manipulations of narrative, time, language, and emotion create a voice that often seems sincere and mocking at the same time. To cite just one significant example, Eggers and Toph play Frisbee together at the beginning, midpoint, and end of the text. These episodes serve as important moments for assessing the relationship between the two brothers and their attitudes toward their environment. One thing that remains constant, however, is Eggers's seemingly high estimation of their throwing skills. At the end of chapter 2, Eggers and Toph arrive at the beach, and Eggers describes their game: "when we throw the world stops and gasps. We throw so far, and with such accuracy, and with such ridiculous beauty. We are perfection, harmony, young and lithe" (67). As the author continues to praise their talents over the next several pages, it becomes increasingly difficult to read the passage literally. Yet the author does not directly challenge the narrator's perspective or provide an explicit counterpoint from which to judge it. In other words, it is difficult to pin down exactly what message the author is attempting to convey. Is the contemporary novelist attempting to describe his former perspective on their Frisbee throwing? And does the contemporary narrator use such overstated language to emphasize his own distance from this attitude? Or is it an attempt to capture the conflicts and contradictions of conscience that characterized his youth? Was the younger Eggers both excessively proud of his throwing ability and also aware of how silly and exaggerated his pride was? Alternatively, does this approach reflect a deeper criticism of exaggeration in general? Or is the author simply declaring, against all common sense, that he actually believes their throwing will make "religious people fall to their knees" (69)?

In short, Eggers comes across as self-deprecating, but he does not offer an explicit alternative to the exaggerated claims of his narrator. As a result, it is fair to say, as Siegel does, that Eggers seems to promote a "modest self-mocking decency" in the book. However, the wild flights of imagination and exaggerated bravado that fill the text cannot simply be dismissed as defensive counterpoint. They are as much a part of the fabric of this story and its narrator as the self-deprecating commentary. Moreover, the book does not end by celebrating a measured form of decency. The narrator's erratic voice becomes more unstable as he wades through increasingly traumatic moments leading up to the final explosive rant that concludes the book.

The difficult tone of the work is also exacerbated by the narrator's sense of himself as an actor. He frequently muses about the "roles" that he is asked to play, as brother, parent (to Toph), friend, employee, writer. At a parent-teacher conference, Eggers is approached by a mother who asks about his relationship with Toph. Their conversation is written in dialogue form, with the name of the speaker centered on the page and the line spoken written beneath it, to emphasize the alienating routine of their words. He even includes a musical staff to capture the exact pitch of the woman's voice when she coos, "What a good brother you are!" (103).

As with most aspects of the book, Eggers sense of himself as an actor is loosely connected with several potential causes, most notably the fact that he is literally presenting himself to a public through the autobiography. He also attributes his feelings to his own distinct psychology and his fascination with watching people, his mother's seemingly omnipotent awareness, and a sense of guilt that has been deeply engrained by his Catholic upbringing, a guilt that makes him both acutely conscious and suspicious of his own actions and motivations. If all of these factors lead Eggers to analyze himself from an external perspective, he also suggests that this tendency has been caused by his experience growing up in the consumer-driven, media-saturated culture of the late-twentieth-century United States. His middle-class immersion in this culture has left him haunted by "echoes from these things having been done before" (270). As a result, he regularly uses television shows and consumer products to explain his experiences. Driving into San Francisco, he says the city looks like "thousands of Lite Brite tubes stuck through the night's paper black" (128). When pursuing a group of people that he mistakenly believes has stolen his wallet, Eggers refers to *Captain America, 21 Jump Street,* and *Baretta.*

As might be expected, Eggers often seems ambivalent about his relationship to this culture. In more positive moods, he embraces the resonances wholeheartedly: "instead of lamenting the end of unmediated experience, I will *celebrate* it, revel in the simultaneous living of an experience and its dozen or so echoes in art and media, the echoes making the experience not cheaper but *richer* . . . not soul-sucking or numbing but edifying, ramifying" (270). This celebration of complexity, of the "ramifying" or branching of pure experience into multiple copies and perspectives, recalls his earlier celebration of artifice in autobiography. This work is simply one limited perspective on a series of events reconstructed at one particular moment in history, a skin long since shed and replaced by other perspectives and possibilities.

However, at other points in the text, Eggers is quick to point out the small-minded bigotries and coarsely manufactured sentimentality promoted by many of the products that he implicitly celebrates. His reluctance to provide an inspirational speech for his suicidal friend, or at least a formulaic version of that speech as echoed by countless television shows and movies, serves as just one example of these reservations. Eggers is often as quick to criticize conventional attitudes as he is to embrace them.

The conflict is readily apparent in his account of *Might.* Many of the pieces from the magazine that he discusses critique conventional media representations, as when they run pictures of various people in their underwear. Eggers explains that their work is "a response to a familiar complaint, of course: the media's and advertising's distortion of our perceptions of our own bodies, how the average person does not and cannot meet the unattainable expectations rammed down our blah blah blah" (247). This account draws the reader's attention to the effect that media can have on subjective perception while simultaneously distancing the narrator from it with a dismissive "blah blah blah." Again, the exact nature of the criticism is left open ended.

Is the author simply redirecting the focus so as not to prolong his blatant sermonizing? Or is it, as the opening "of course" might suggest, a criticism of the conventionality of this posture? Or is it a criticism of the larger idea that this "exercise," as Eggers calls it, was meant to convey?

The author's potential dismissal is further complicated by the sheer number of such "exercises" that he discusses in the text. He details numerous pieces from *Might* throughout the second half of the book, many of which could be categorized as more or less conventional cultural critiques. Eggers's campaign to fake the death of the former child star Adam Rich, the actor who played Nicholas on *Eight Is Enough,* amounts to little more than a broad satire of media interest in and coverage of celebrity deaths.

Eggers's cultural critiques are also complicated by other facets of the text. The Rich stunt, for instance, is recounted amidst Eggers's ongoing anxieties about his own attempt to turn his parents' deaths into a touching book. In addition, Eggers, as he does throughout the story, questions his own motives for publishing these pieces. Toph, again serving as a representative of conscience, breaks out of character late in the book to challenge the premise that they are working with Rich to challenge the media: "can it be any more gruesome and transparently symbolic, you people killing this contemporary of yours . . . who you claim is in on it all but who really has no idea of the scale of, the potential consequences of this thing—and certainly not your motivations, the bitterness simmering just below the surface, the desire to dirty him, humiliate him, reduce him to you, to below you" (316–17).

In short, Eggers incorporates *Might* pieces into the text in part for their humorous appeal, and through them he critiques aspects of American culture. At the same time, he distances himself from and possibly even dismisses the attitudes and motivations that the magazine represents. The primary and most often repeated charge he levels at his former endeavor is that, regardless of any other motives he and his friends might have had, they were always thinking about self-promotion. In its short run, for instance, *Might* formed alliances with several political organizations that aimed to mobilize twenty-somethings, including Lead or Leave and Third Millennium. Yet, Eggers admits, "we have absolutely no idea what they're talking about . . . what we are most interested in is their mailing list" (174–75). Toph, in his criticism of the Adam Rich endeavor, emphatically levels the same charge: "you feel, deep down, that because there is no life before or after this, that fame is, essentially, God" (317).

The subject of fame appears quite prominently in Eggers's meditations on contemporary culture and serves, in part, as a unifying theme that connects different and seemingly unrelated aspects of the work. If the book as a whole documents Eggers's attempt to deal with his parents' deaths and to create a new life with his younger brother, it also represents his bid for public recognition, recognition cultivated through revelations about his family and friends. Eggers's quest for recognition also helps to motivate stretches of action in the story, including his work on *Might* and his effort to get on *The Real World*, a popular reality show on MTV. At the literal heart of the book, the sixth of eleven sections, is a long, though admittedly faked, transcript of Eggers's interview as part of his effort to get on the show.

In characteristic fashion, the narrator is simultaneously fascinated and appalled by *The Real World*. It promises to portray the "real" lives of young men and women but only in a carefully engineered, if not fully scripted, environment that is certain to capture a cross section of views and values. Such a platform would allow Eggers to tell his story, but only at the risk of being turned into a primetime caricature. In a comment that echoes some of the statements Eggers makes about his own text, he says that the show has a "strange ability to flatten all the depth and nuance from these people" (209).

Because of the show's suspect cultural status, none of his friends will even admit to watching it, and Eggers must couch his own application as a publicity stunt for *Might*. In his version of the interview, however, he begs the woman to let him on the show so that he can share his story. He even offers to tailor his performance to fit the producer's needs. At the end of the interview, Eggers pleads his case, suggesting that the contradictions present in him make him a perfect candidate for reaching a mass audience: "I am the common multiplier for 47 million! I am the perfect amalgam! I was born of both stability and chaos. I have seen nothing and everything. I am twenty-four but feel then thousand years old. I am emboldened by youth, unfettered and hopeful, though inextricably tied to the past and future by my beautiful brother, who is part of both? Can you not see that we're extraordinary?" (236).

The theme of fame bridges Eggers's meditations on contemporary culture and his more abstract musings about genre, truth, and visibility. It also appears in even more personal elements of the text, such as the death of his mother. Eggers is constantly worried about using her passing as fodder for his own self-promotion. At the same time, he seems to imagine the book as a tribute to her, a monument to her unrecognized generosity. In the second to last chapter in the book, he revisits the church where her funeral service was held and rages about the scant turnout: "This is the crowd that was at my *father's*. It should not be the same crowd, the same number. . . . She fought for so long for all you people, she fought every day, she fought everything, fought for every breath until the last . . . she grabbed at the air, grabbed for us and for you, and where are you?" (406).

Throughout the book, the importance of fame changes with Eggers's mood. It variously represents an acknowledgment of a person's skill or value, an avenue for connection, a way of acquiring power, and an opportunity to share and potentially diminish pain. His feelings about public recognition change almost as frequently. At the extremes, he vacillates between championing the idea that "anonymity is existentially irrational, indefensible" (202) and bemoaning the feeling that he is always "inside a fishbowl," even when he is alone in his house (212).

As the book nears its end, Eggers's emotions become, if anything, even more complicated. He continues to reveal his anger at the world around him, at his parents, and at himself. This suppressed rage is exacerbated and complicated by a pervasive sense of guilt about the anger and the revelations contained in the memoir. He also becomes increasingly haunted by his own inability to connect with others, which is reflected in his anger at the audience and his many failed personal and sexual encounters in the book. All of this is overlaid with Eggers's own self-conscious musings, which often raise possible connections and explanations without seeming to impose an authoritative perspective on the text.

It is, finally, a complex and contradictory book that provides few concrete answers. As *Might* prepares to fold and Eggers and Toph plan to move again, the exhausted narrator can offer little more than pragmatic resignation. In the final issue of *Might,* he writes, "Seasons change, love withers, the good die young/ . . . It is, of course, easy to say these things, just as it is easy to, say, watch a lot of television. But, easy or not, we rely on such sentiment. To do otherwise would be to jump without hope into a black and endless abyss" (417). In the book's closing moments, Eggers hopes to say something that transcends the clichés of contemporary culture, but, at the same time, he acknowledges that this culture has necessarily shaped his own thoughts. Without it and the rules and limitations that he rails against throughout the book, he would have nothing. In short, this "abyss" becomes a counterpoint to the joyous world of unfettered creation that Eggers imagines in better moods. He can continue to look for truth and push for originality but must acknowledge that his search will be carried out in and through the mundane platitudes that circulate in his culture. The tone here is darker, but Eggers still clings to his idealistic hope that "we can play it both ways, all ways" (245).

In the end, *A Heartbreaking Work of Staggering Genius* provides a complex and powerful meditation on human endurance. Eggers struggles with the deaths of his parents and the responsibilities that their passing thrusts upon him, even as he wrestles with guilt and anxiety over the ways that he responds to these events. The whole situation is complicated further by the present-tense perspective of the book, that is, the added layer of anxieties felt by the author as he sets out to capture his painful ordeals on the page. In its restlessness and confusion, *A Heartbreaking Work of Staggering Genius* attempts to capture the complexity of contemporary middle-class life and the challenges that can emerge even in the richest and most homogeneous suburbs. Throughout the work, Eggers joins a slippery theatricality with a surprising frankness. He champions sincerity by admitting his secrecy. He maintains a sense of himself as utterly ordinary and yet feels ordained by his tragic circumstances. At the end of his acknowledgments, Eggers suggests a figure from popular culture that might serve as a symbolic analog for his troubled protagonist: the comic-book superhero. He defines this figure as "the normal, mild-mannered person transformed into mutant by freak accident, with the mutant thereafter driven by a strange hybrid of the most rancid bitterness and the most outrageous hope to do very, very odd and silly things, many times in the name of Good. The makers of comic books seemed to be onto something there" (xliii). This description might only loosely fit many comic-book superheroes, but it does capture some of the crucial tensions that emerge over the course of the book. It also appropriately emphasizes the complex emotions that drive the plot forward, even when those tensions seem irresolvable.

CHAPTER 3

You Shall Know Our Velocity

Eggers published his first novel, *You Shall Know Our Velocity,*[1] just two years after the release of *A Heartbreaking Work of Staggering Genius.* The book tells the story of two twenty-somethings, Will Chmielewski and his friend Hand. At the outset of the story, the two are planning to travel around the world in one week and, along the way, hand out $38,000 that Will unexpectedly received from an ad agency. (Through a random sequence of events, a photo of Will screwing in a light bulb was turned into a logo for a light bulb manufacturer.)

In the frantic opening pages, the two men, driven by Will's insistence that they leave *now,* sit down to plot out their grand journey. Logistical difficulties abound. Neither one of them, for instance, has a visa. They also want to travel off the beaten path and incorporate as much variety into the trip as they can. Their first agenda (Mongolia, Qatar, Yemen, Madagascar, Rwanda) turns out to be "too warm, too concentrated in one latitude" (5). The second itinerary overcompensates and winds up including too many places that are too cold. As logistical problems and schedule conflicts multiply, they run through several more agendas without finding one that is "just right." The two finally agree to a rough outline: begin in Greenland and end on top of a pyramid in Egypt. The rest of the trip will be improvised. The travelers throw together supplies that seem to parody traditional tourist trappings, including seven hundred pages ripped out of a biography of Winston Churchill and a "sheaf of papers" from the Center for Disease Control that are "almost entirely about ebola" (21). They also purchase disposable clothing that can be worn in layers and discarded along the way (21).

It does not take long for even this streamlined plan to fall apart. After oversleeping, the two speed off to the airport, only to find out that their flight to Greenland has been canceled. They quickly change plans and get tickets to Dakar. (Will has to check his atlas to find out that the city is in Senegal.) Then their second flight of the day is postponed for eight hours, and the whole crowd is shuffled off to a local Best Western, a fitting beginning to a week full of delays and deferrals. Their whirlwind trip around the world is ultimately reduced to a small sampling of Senegal, Morocco, Estonia, and Latvia. The two never make it to the pyramids, and when they are able to follow through on a plan, things rarely turn out the way they expect.

Still, the travelers press on in hope of seeing the world and giving away money to strangers. The biggest question hanging over the opening pages of the text is why? In part the answer is obscured by the psychology of the characters involved. Will, who announces in the opening paragraph that he will drown in Colombia after the close of the story, narrates in the first person. He provides basic information about his past early on in the story, but, like the narrator in *A Heartbreaking Work of Staggering Genius,* he wrestles with past traumas throughout the text and slowly reveals crucial details as the story develops. This bit of fictional artifice, the measured revelation of information throughout the story, is further complicated by Will's psychological instability. In some of the earliest moments depicted, Will describes a period of his childhood when he decided to "become a better human" by eliminating emotion. He says, "I spoke in a monotone. I could not be excited and could not be upset. . . . I was not sullen; I was predictable. I walked at a normal human pace" (150).

One night, as Hand sleeps, Will imagines the two of them in a discussion about this period. "Hand" repeatedly argues that this episode was linked to Will's father, who is obliquely described in the text as a figure that flitted in and out of Will's life. Will denies the connection and instead links the change in his behavior to the diagnosis of a heart condition that causes him to lose consciousness periodically. Despite his insistence that this stint as "Robotman," as Hand calls it, had nothing to do with his father, he recounts several traumatic moments from his childhood, including the time his father fell off a balcony and landed on his mother and the night he watched his mother cry on the phone as she told her friends that her ex-husband had walked out of their lives again.

In the present moment of the text, Will is also haunted by numerous other events in his life, such as the time that he, Hand, and their other close childhood friend, Jack, set a cow on fire. His current emotional crisis, however, was triggered by more recent events. Six months before the opening of the novel, Jack died in a car accident. To make matters worse, Will and Hand are forced to clean out their friend's storage locker. Before they begin, Hand picks a fight with a man in the gas station across the street from the storage facility. The man leaves, but, a short while later, a group of men show up at the lockers. Hand has wandered off to explore a National Guard armory nearby, so Will is alone inside the locker. He is savagely beaten and left unconscious on the floor.

As the novel begins, Will is struggling with abandonment (by his father, Jack, Hand) and the collective horrors that crowd his consciousness. Much like the narrator of *A Heartbreaking Work of Staggering Genius,* Will is prone to imaginative visions. He pictures his mind as a vast underground file system run by "a large staff of humanoid people, oily and pale and without hair—they are moles and look like it, with huge square yellow teeth and mouths of fire" (30). While the system normally works well, staff members have recently been bringing up the most traumatic files without any prompting. To make matters worse, Will believes that his "mind has an uncanny knack for organization when it comes to pain. Nothing tormenting is lost, never even diminished in color or intensity or quality of sound. These were filed near the front" (30).

One of Will's solutions, and part of the impetus for the journey, is movement itself. Early in the text, Will provides a generic explanation for his desire to travel. It will be a time of "unmitigated movement, of serving any or maybe every impulse" (9). When pressed by voices in his head later in the text, he elaborates: "The only times [the horrible thoughts] are not with me are those times when speed overwhelms, when the action of moments supersedes and crowds out. When my movements stop they come. When my eyes are fixed they come" (147). As with most of Will's plans, his effort to outrun past traumas works only intermittently, and the text as a whole moves erratically through genuine bursts of speed to long stretches of waiting (in airports, hotels, and bars) to Will's brooding internal monologues.

Certainly part of the problem is that Will himself has only the vaguest ideas about what he is doing and seems to have very little direct control over much that goes on in his head. The mole people keep bringing him files at inopportune moments, and at times he insists that someone else altogether "borrows" his head. Will is also prone to internal debates with people around him. Initially, he describes these conversations as "silent though decisive discussions" that help him "work through problems, solving things." When he chastises a Lexus driver for having an overpriced car, the driver in his head simply responds, "You are right. I have failed but will repent" (27). As Will begins to work through his difficulties throughout the text, however, the voices in his head begin raising questions that he cannot easily answer.

If *A Heartbreaking Work of Staggering Genius* also dramatizes the narrator's limited knowledge and documents a painful process of self-reflection, Eggers's first book is more explicitly concerned with its own creation. Beyond internal monologues, the narrator's uncertainties are most strikingly dramatized in ways that call attention to the construction of the book itself, as in the prefatory materials or the metafictional debates about the story and its motivations. In *You Shall Know Our Velocity,* Will has similar debates with other characters, but they are explicitly situated in his head, an internalization that emphasizes individual psychology much more directly than in the previous book. This shift also draws greater attention to Will's lack of control. The horrible memories and voices of disagreement that plague Will are products of his own brain and not an external character (even if the external character is little more than the materialization of his own thoughts, as in *A Heartbreaking Work of Staggering Genius*). These debates are explicitly positioned as internal struggles, and they show Will groping toward a greater awareness of himself and the world around him.

His emotional and psychological limitations at the beginning of the text are also apparent in the vague and often contradictory justifications he initially gives for his actions. To explain the project of giving away money, for instance, he simply says that it will "provide clarity" (4). Yet Will also feels guilty about his relatively privileged position in the world, feels unsettled by the randomness of his earnings, and claims that he is "much more comfortable living on the equator just above and below a zero balance" (15). Additionally, when he stops to consider how the trip and his philanthropy are linked, he is forced to admit, "I really don't know why we combined these two ideas" (4). These two impulses could go together, as flip sides of a seize-the-day/embrace-the-world narrative. Yet they are also defined at certain points in the text as contradictory enterprises. One is motivated by hedonistic impulses ("serving any or maybe every impulse") and the other by a desire to serve humanity. Perhaps the literary critic Aliki Varvogli best captures Eggers's characteristic ambivalence by pointing out that neither extreme adequately captures the reality of the story. Will and Hand's "half-baked, ill executed scheme is neither genuine philanthropy nor self-indulgence," even if their endeavors occasionally approach each position.[2]

If Will's vague explanations and his internal conflicts reveal profound psychological difficulties, they also suggest the limitations of his perspective. The voices in Will's head often provide competing and contradictory positions that he must acknowledge as he comes to terms with his life. At moments, they even suggest the possibility that Will is completely misreading particular situations. Will, for instance, often describes Jack in a way that sets him apart from the other two friends. Jack was the calm one, the one who was settled and happy in his life, the one who refused to speed. (Jack dies after a speeding truck runs him over from behind.) Will also imagines Jack as an unwilling participant in some of their childhood antics. Most significant, Jack, Will reassures himself, resisted their plan to set the cow on fire. The imaginary voice of Hand, however, quickly rejects this interpretation ("he stayed because he wanted to" [261]).

The actual Hand serves a similar function in the text by providing a second point of view that complicates and often obliquely challenges Will's version of events. When Will mentions giving away money for the first time, he says that "purging would provide clarity" (4). Yet, just before they leave for the trip, Hand questions Will's motives and says, "I don't want you doing this as some weird purging bullshit thing. This doesn't have anything to do with anything" (11). Will passively agrees, but the issue resurfaces at several points throughout the text, as both men struggle to understand the meaning of their actions.

To make matters worse, the text is littered with obvious factual mistakes, from subtle changes in details to small shifts in time. These inconsistencies underscore Will's unreliability and contribute to the novel's larger construction of an unpredictable world. These two young men operate in a seemingly random universe that offers them little hope of control. Accordingly, the action is punctuated by events that the two are at a loss to explain. Early in the text, a uniformed man jumps into their car and starts directing them around the city for no apparent reason. Later, a man in a hotel bar yells "Heil Hitler!" before walking out.

This interpretation is complicated somewhat by Will and Hand's lack of knowledge about their surroundings. Their general ignorance raises the possibility that a larger order could exist. That order might simply lie beyond the protagonists' ability to perceive it. So, in a fairly conventional postmodern maneuver, the text holds out the possibility of closure even as, in practice, truth is always deferred, displaced, or otherwise denied.

As in *A Heartbreaking Work of Staggering Genius,* the tone of the book, which hovers almost impossibly between self-parody and unabashed sincerity, manages to contain these uncertainties even as it complicates the perspective of the text as a whole. Hand and Will often seem to be absurd characters, young men who plan a trip around the world before stopping to consider that they might need visas. On other continents, they try to tape money to donkeys and worry about the authentic appearance of a treasure map drawn up on graph paper, a map they hope will lead some lucky child to a wad of foreign currency buried beneath a dagger. While these imaginative and deliberately ridiculous antics are a great source of humor in the book, it is also possible to step back and laugh directly *at* these characters for their confused bumbling. At the same time, Will is explicitly aware of many of his limitations, and he admirably struggles against them in his efforts to make a difference. To follow this line just one step further, Will is also painfully aware that his efforts might not come to anything, might in fact backfire because of complex social and historical conditions that he is not equipped to understand. In a reflexive meditation on commitment, the author Wen Stephenson sums up what he calls the "post-postmodern" sensibility of the story: "We recognize ourselves in Will and Hand's absurd antics. . . . They want so badly to believe, IN SPITE OF THEMSELVES, that human connection, understanding—belief itself!—is possible. So Eggers lets us laugh at ourselves —nervously, of course, conscious of the self-flattery it implies—and yet take him, and ourselves, seriously at the same time."[3]

This complex attitude is central to Eggers's first two texts, which both track the vicissitudes of a certain kind of contemporary self-awareness. *You Shall Know Our Velocity* expands the scope of the project in part by moving its brooding, white midwestern men outside the familiar confines of the United States. As might be expected in a work focused on two relatively sheltered young men, the book opens with references to stereotypical binaries (East/West, self/other, us/them). In the opening pages, Will paces nervously from the "western edge" of his apartment to the far east side, as he tries to convince Hand over the phone to travel around the world with him the following week. When talking with their travel agent in Fort Collins, Colorado, Will imagines the city as an actual fort, "hewn from area lumber and still walling the pioneers from the natives" (10). For Will, who is nervous about being set apart by his white skin or his large stack of traveler's checks, the world consists of the United States and then "all other nations . . . huddled together, trading information and commiserating, like smokers outside a building" (52).

Yet, as the two begin to travel, they are surprised by the extent to which things outside the United States seem familiar. Much of the music they hear, on the radio or in clubs, is American. They never travel far without finding someone who speaks English. Landscapes repeatedly remind them of home: "Estonia could look like Nebraska . . . Kansas like Morocco. Morocco like Arles. On and On. Growing up I thought all countries looked, were required to look, completely different. . . . But every country now seemed to offer a little of every other country, and every given landscape, I finally realized, existed somewhere in the U.S." (253–54). The literary scholar Caren Irr, in a survey of twenty-first-century expatriate writing, argues that this is one way in which contemporary travel writing is different from its early twentieth-century predecessors. In earlier writings, Americans abroad devoted great attention to the "local particularities of place and scene," documenting the newness of their surroundings. Within this "alien" landscape, the hero, often seeking to escape the constraints and limitations of home, could be "temporarily and therapeutically released." In contrast, contemporary works such as *You Shall Know Our Velocity* present "a relatively continuous, tendentiously homogeneous world space" that emphasizes "the inescapability of the cultural matrix of origin."[4]

This movement away from both absolute oppositions and a hero who can clearly perceive cultural difference helps to keep the focus of the text on the narrator's often-murky subjectivity. The book is ultimately less about what happens when one culture, defined as a knowable and static thing, collides with another culture than it is about the way in which Will perceives and interprets the world around him. His idiosyncratic perspective and limited knowledge or, perhaps more directly, his awareness of his limited knowledge colors everything in the text, creating a slippery world that seems to transform with each new reflection or shift in mood. After a man from Tallinn contradicts their guidebook, Will boldly asserts, "The word *fact* could not exist. All facts changed on the way to the printer" (272).

Though Will seems predisposed to this conclusion from the beginning of the book, he does not immediately embrace the fluidity that he repeatedly notes in the world around him. The death of his friend and his own chance beating have left him desiring "only *truth,* as simple as you could serve it, straight down the middle, not the product of dialectic but *sui generis:* Truth!" (27). Later, Will even admits to fantasizing about car crashes and other horrible accidents as a way of limiting his future possibilities: "I wanted to land on my head and lose half of it, or land on my legs and lose one or both—I wanted something to happen so my choices would be fewer, so my map would have a route straight through, in red" (302–3).

Throughout the book, Will lugs around part of a biography of Winston Churchill, a man whose life seems, at least to Will, to revolve around a clear and direct purpose. In one imaginary conversation, he says, "Mr. Churchill, you were given a mission. . . . I want to have been given your mission. I want your place in world events, the centrality of it. You were born in the cradle of a catapult!" (181). In contrast, Will and Hand meander with only the vaguest of purposes, pushed by desires and feelings that they do not entirely understand toward ends that are themselves not entirely clear. Even the project of giving away money, a seemingly simple act of generosity with a clear moral value, becomes the subject of a running debate throughout the book.

Part of this debate takes place in Will's head. After he refuses to give a boy some money because his desire is too transparent, an imaginary version of the boy chides Will: "you want docility. You want me to appear indifferent to the money. . . . And as a reward I am given my share. . . . This is shameful. . . . You want the control money provides" (117). Other portions of the debate are carried on with Will's mother, whom he periodically calls throughout the journey. Several pages later, she reiterates the boy's charges, asking if their "subjective" method of distribution is unfair and, ultimately, condescending (123). Will becomes enraged at her questioning and is clearly disturbed by the ease with which a seemingly benevolent act can so easily be turned against him. After a long rant in his head, Will moves to cut off such questioning: "I just think you're overthinking it, Mom" (124).

In contrast to this complex and slippery rationalizing, he yearns for something "accountable above" (86). In short, he wants to live in a universe where his suffering is retribution for the wrong that he has done to others. This impulse is connected to his desire to see others who have wronged be punished, including his father, the trucker who killed Jack, the people who beat him up, and the undertaker who could not properly reconstruct Jack's face. Through much of the text, he clings to a notion of cosmic balance in a universe where "Everything lives in perfect Newtonian opposition" (147). However, given the way that Will describes the world throughout much of the text, this vision seems to be motivated more by hope than by a genuine belief in an ordered universe. Even the voices in his own head understand the deep desires that motivate Will's conceptions. The imaginary voice of Hand explains, "You're pleading for punishment in hopes that you'll see your God. Without punishment there is no God. If there is balance then there is your Lord. Balance then afterlife" (263).

Will's desires are traced back in part to his father's love of the Old Testament. Will cannot say for certain if his father was religious; his family never attended church. Yet his dad used to read aloud from a marked-up copy of the Old Testament. The novel, which is presumably Will's writing, is also full of references to the New Testament. After Will is beaten, suffering in one sense *for* his friend, Hand takes one look at his friend and says, "Jesus fucking Christ" (91). Yet, as Will moves away from the idea of a balanced universe with a retributive God, he also turns away from any wholesale acceptance of Christian teachings. In an obvious biblical parallel, Will and Hand leave Marrakesh to travel up the Atlas Mountains. Will later admits that he was listening for directions there. God, however, does not speak. What is more, Will is not even certain that they reached the top of the mountain.

In contrast to this confused search for answers on a silent mountain, he praises a frantic drive through the city streets below. While racing past groups of people in narrow alleys, unsure whether they are being followed by robbers, Will and Hand experience a powerful charge. There was, Will claims, "Reason! Purpose! A love born of caring that we were there!" At the end of an eight-page meditation, he concludes, "Jack I'm sorry. But we're not going up there again, to that mountain, or maybe any mountain, again" (304–5). This decision reflects Will's movement away from a certain kind of idealism toward immediate experience. After their near-death experience and the descent from the mountain, Will begins encouraging them to take leaps, as from a moving car to a donkey-driven cart or from one tree to another. These are exhilarating secular versions of the leap of faith that he cannot make. Will also becomes more explicit in his embrace of the physical world. Late in the novel, he lays down on the edge of a sheet of ice to feel the water: "The water was not God. The water undulating slightly with the waves unformed was not spiritual. It was jagged cold water, and it felt perfect when we put our hand into it . . . and why wasn't that enough?" (339). With this final question, the ice breaks, and Will is metaphorically baptized by the material world.

In the seemingly random and ever-changing universe in which they travel, a world where "all facts changed on the way to the printer," Will also comes to insist on the importance of firsthand experience: "even if we knew something, had read something, were almost sure of something, we wouldn't ever know the truth, or come anywhere close to it. The truth had to be seen. Anything else was a story, entertaining but more embroidered fib than crude, shapeless fact" (238–39). While this insistence on the importance of the material present could serve as a retreat from complexity, Will does not deny the necessity of creating his own "embroidered fibs" any more than he denies the complex sociohistorical networks that structure individual experience. Individual interpretation is, from this perspective, always shaped by complex psychological and social factors, but it must begin with one's own vision and not the stories of others. Engaging the world through primary experience, Will says in a postcard to his nieces, is not a retreat. It only makes things more complicated (228).

This complication results in part from the fact that truth is, according to the narrator, impossible to acquire. Accordingly, the protagonists' attempts to find clear answers or even a remnant of an older, more "authentic" world repeatedly fail. The two plan to stop at the end of their journey, for instance, and give away the last of their money to the Liv, members of a five-thousand-year-old Finno-Ugric fishing tribe that still inhabits the Gulf of Riga. Elders there, Will learns from his guidebook, could still speak an ancient Livonian tongue. The travelers never make it and wind up hurling bills out of the car windows as they race to the airport. Similarly, the title of the novel comes from a message left by an ancient tribe in South America, the Jumping People. Yet even this line, "you shall know our velocity," turns out to be a scholarly interpretation. The message has, Hand points out, been translated and retranslated so many times that it is no longer possible to reconstruct the original (327).

Instead of advocating a "return" to origins or some form of simplistic escapism, Will is far more committed to the cultivation of individual perspective. As in *A Heartbreaking Work of Staggering Genius,* in which the narrator fantasizes about reconstructing the world from scratch every day, Will imaginatively rebels against the constraints he perceives in the conventional flows of everyday life. Both Will and Hand celebrate randomness on their journey as they walk into a stranger's house with a bouquet of flowers or pay cab drivers large sums of money to simply drive them around in a circle. Through these actions, Will hopes, in part, to fill others with a sense of wonder and promise. He champions creative possibilities in a way that is both deliberately ridiculous and totally sincere. As Will says after a series of ten-second cab rides, "none of it really meant anything, or meant everything but in a way we wouldn't ever really understand" (208). Even Will's imaginary Winston Churchill rebels against simple historical determinism, advocating the power of individuals to cultivate their own destiny. In response to the charge that he was simply born at a crucial moment and had his mission dictated to him by external events, Churchill replies, "You are wrong. I found my mission" (181).

Will and Hand's random missions also serve as ways to create connections between people. Will imagines being lectured by a stripper, who insists that both of them are motivated to transform "the limits of normal human relations—chilly, clothed, circumscribed. Our hearts pull against their leashes" (242). Throughout the text, Will insists on his desire to develop connections with others, despite his own instinct to withdraw. One of the larger ironies hanging over the narrative is that Will blames others (his father, Hand) for not being there when he needed them. Yet Will himself has largely retreated into his own head at the beginning of the story and has a long history of hiding, both literally and emotionally, from others.

Over the course of the book, he does become more willing to reach out and gradually learns to navigate the anxieties that lead him to retreat. Early in the text, for instance, he and Hand leave a couple of women in a café. As they go, Will regrets not offering them any money but still gives them only "the tight, smarmy smile I give to homeless people when I have nothing for them" (66). By the end of the text, he is able to chase a family down without Hand around and give them a handful of traveler's checks. Similarly, he goes from drinking alone while others dance to bouncing around sober with an old friend in the closing pages of the book.

As Will's outlook changes, he runs across a series of people who offer alternate perspectives, visions that might replace the absolutism that Will at least superficially champions at points in the text. One comes from a Parisian woman named Annette, who joins Will and Hand for a late-night swim in Dakar. While the three float in the water, she explains that they are all searching for the "Fourth World" here, alone together at night in a strange location. By seeing this "setting and moment as whole," outside everyday existence and the narratives of ordinary life, they can arrive at a "staging ground." This place, "half thought, half actual," is where they "create things that will happen" (141). Annette's mystical vision of an alternate space from which to generate new possibilities for the world is both appealing to Will, who mentions it periodically throughout the remainder of the text, and a bit absurd. When Annette tells him to "forget about momentum and start again, and again," she repeats the word "again" "about a dozen times." Even Will, mesmerized by her beauty and sincerely struggling to follow her abstract vision, concedes that "she was a little batty" (141).

Similarly, Will and Hand run across a Chilean man named Raymond who believes that he is descended from an ancient tribe that subsequently came to be called the Jumping People. In contrast to the "wispy ghost" of a soul imagined by many Westerners, these people believed that they carry the souls of all their ancestors inside them in a dense spiritual mountain. To counteract the weight of these massive souls, they worshipped birds, who, the Jumping People imagined, functioned like balloons, as vessels for gases. Accordingly, they darted and jumped around with their mouths open, collecting gases that, at the very least, would lighten their spiritual loads. (For a while, they entertained the hope that these gases might accumulate over generations and allow them to fly.) When the conquistadors arrived and besieged their main village, the Jumping People relied on their speed and simply dispersed. On the cliff above their village, they scrawled one final message: "YOU SHALL KNOW OUR VELOCITY!" (319–28).

Again, this vision appeals to Will, who has been relishing speed and feels the "impermanence of place" (327). It also promotes a new perspective on memory. As Hand points out, modern Westerners live with the "illusion that we want to forget things . . . because everything is too much, our burdens are so great we need to self-lobotomize. . . . But these people want to carry around everything and everyone" (322). The Jumping People are not "irrelevant and unbound" (304), as Will fears that he will be unless he starts connecting with others. They are able to contain the voices of history and speak with the weight of a whole bloodline.

All of these perspectives are complicated by Will's ambivalent attitude. He is clearly attracted to portions of these positions, even as he acknowledges their limitations, contradictions, and absurdities. Hand's whole account of the Jumping People, for instance, is sprinkled with Will's questioning and often dismissive comments. The story is also offset by details of the two men wandering around the city looking for landmarks to guide them. In one telling moment, they even pass a cheese shop, suggesting that this fantastic ten-page story remembered from a conversation, perhaps under the influence, in the middle of night days earlier is not meant to be taken with absolute seriousness (324).

Moreover, the positions that Will does seem attracted to are often obviously problematic or at least more complex than Will's momentary celebrations suggest. While he ends the text by reaffirming the power of the fourth world, saying that he hopes to take his mother there, he uses the same language of staging and creation to describe one of the most horrific events in the book, their childhood cow burning: "I had a vision of a cow on fire and we decided we had to make that vision real. We had no right" (261). Similarly, Will's desire to affirm the present moment, which at points suggests a complex mediation of thought and action, at other points is linked to Will's desire for a more simplistic world. Part of the reason he likes life in the city below the mountain, as noted in the earlier example, is that "there were few options and with few options comes such great solace" (302).

In short, the text does not move forward in a direct, linear way. Will's progress is contested and fragmentary, and he struggles to assemble a new worldview from portions of the events and fictions that he encounters on the trip. Even moments that seem to mark genuine leaps forward are fraught with self-conscious questioning and quick regressions. When Will has to re-explain to Hand why they are giving the money away, an explanation that is itself noticeably absent from the text, he says, "Always we learned things and forgot them. Almost nothing could be learned for good" (239).

The story as a whole can be viewed similarly, as a self-conscious assemblage of various genres that never wholly encapsulate the narrative, much as any one genre might resonate through certain scenes or strands of plot. It is a buddy novel and a road trip documentary, a belated coming-of-age story and an account of coming to terms with grief, an existential meditation on existence and an allegory about contemporary humanitarian intervention, a quest for atonement and a reaffirmation of life. Eggers calls attention to these various strands through stylistic allusions and overt references to work by authors such as Saul Bellow, Ernest Hemingway, Jack Kerouac, J. D. Salinger, and Mark Twain. Similarly, the text is littered with motifs and symbols that are evocative but incomplete. Will's and Hand's names present an obvious example. On some levels, these names are fitting. Will spends much of the text dwelling on his internal dynamics and also serves as the prime motivator for the trip, while the active connotations of "hand" reflect the character's extroverted nature and impulsiveness. One reviewer even shorthanded these connections with simple parentheticals: "Will (thought)" and "Hand (action)."[5] Yet Hand, as an autodidact who gathers and often distorts unusual details on a wide range of topics, also has a greater investment in information than Will does. Conversely, it could be argued that Will is equally impulsive, since he seems to be blundering into this trip with only the vaguest sense of what he hopes to accomplish. The text as a whole resists the kind of easy closure that such abstract parallels offer, just as it suggests alternate visions that complicate Will's perspective. Will's death even serves as a potential disruption of the larger narrative outlined earlier.

From a slightly different perspective, the novel also hovers between being an earnest account of one man's growth and an almost parodic exploration of arrogant Western interventionism. While the story does put a Westerner's self-absorbed quest for atonement and growth at the center of the text, it also contains a "self-consciousness about the derivativeness of the very project" and a skepticism about easy resolutions.[6] Will is, finally, someone who is struggling to overcome his privilege and to find a new language for encountering the "other," even if his efforts often seem circumscribed by his position and limited in vision. The issue comes up at several moments in the text, as both Hand and Will's mother question where other people fit into his narrative of personal growth. When Will champions Annette's vision of a "staging ground," for instance, Hand replies, "The problem with that idea is that you have to see these other people as—well, how do they figure in? How does that guy in the shop figure in? Is he part of it, or part of the scenery?" (199).

Will gravitates toward the term "chorus" throughout the novel, suggesting either a collective voice or the chorus of Greek drama, those figures who inform and comment on the action of the main characters. This understanding represents an imperfect attempt to reconceptualize the power disparity between Will and those around him without naively dismissing it. Or course, as Will, or at least the voices in his head, would be quick to point out, the attempt is itself a product of Will's privilege, leaving him in an even more abstract and complicated bind.

Ultimately, Will and Hand's trip represents the kind of pragmatic leap that Eggers proposes in *A Heartbreaking Work of Staggering Genius.* A person can exist entirely in the head, lost forever in the moral ambiguities and logical complexities of any particular action. Alternatively, that person can acknowledge those complexities and blunder ahead, never leaving the challenges entirely behind but also not letting them stand in the way of a genuine attempt to reach out. Will opts to reach out, and the story he writes, whether serious or satirical, sympathetic or offensively self-indulgent, reflects his profound desire for change.

You Shall Know Our Velocity was originally put out in 2002 by Eggers's own publishing imprint, McSweeney's, and was distributed through independent bookstores. In early 2003, Eggers and McSweeney's published a new version of the text, titled *Sacrament: Hand's Revised Edition,* which contains, most notably, a section written by Hand after Will's death. A paperback version of the text was released by Vintage during the summer of 2003 with the original title, modified only by the addition of an exclamation mark: *You Shall Know Our Velocity!* The title page notes that the book was "previously retitled as *Sacrament,*" and some, but not all, of the Vintage paperbacks contain Hand's additions.

While Hand's version radically rewrites the narrative of their journey, the text reinforces many of the themes prevalent in Eggers's original text. Hand's section, written "almost two years after the action taking place in this book" (251), is inserted late in the story after Will collapses on the street in Estonia and has to be carried part of the way back to the hotel. (Hand, in a bit of metacommentary reminiscent of *A Heartbreaking Work of Staggering Genius,* claims that this is the point at which he found the plot "waning.") The "Interruption," as it is called, finds Hand watching the rain in New Zealand, where he has sequestered himself to comment on Will's text. One of Hand's issues with the book is that he and Will went into this trip planning to write about it and to convey what happened as honestly as possible. While the final text "tells the plain truth eighty-five percent of the time, day to day, of what we did" (281), it contains a few major distortions. It is also, Hand claims, colored by "innuendo and gesture" that obscure both the characters' motivations and some of the major implications of their trip (252).

First, Hand says that Will's mother died from complications in surgery long before they went on their trip. She certainly was not alive to drown in a Colombian river with Will, as the opening paragraph of the original text claims. (The opening that announces Will's death was written, according to Hand, by a ghostwriter.) Second, Jack never existed. Hand guesses that he was created as a stand-in for Will's dead mother. Third, Will had never been in a fight in his life and was never beaten in a storage facility in Oconomowoc. The facial wounds, which metaphorically represent Will's psychological injuries and often help to distance him from others on their trip, never really existed. Finally, Will had received the $80,000 eight years before their trip and, on their journey, had committed to giving away only half of it.

In this account, the trip around the world was not motivated by any recent death, and the two were not explicitly fleeing anything. Hand admits that Will's "more conventional" narrative might help some readers by providing a clear motivation for their journey (268–69). Their real motivation, however, was probably little more than "shame of contentment" or a desire to reach out to others (274). Hand, consequently, has renamed the text *Sacrament* to recast their trip as a secular version of a sacred rite. It was "an outward symbolic act of an inward grace . . . the external, social demonstration of how we feel within" (287). All of these elements, including the Catholic overtones, are part of the original text, as noted earlier, but they appear alongside discussion of a range of other problems and issues that Will is trying to resolve.

The revised version of Will's story offers no authoritative commentary to help the reader weigh the alternate perspectives presented. Hand's "Interruption" provides just one more account of events. The tension it generates does, however, work with the original text by intensifying the uncertainties present in a more subtle form throughout the story. Hand's version also underscores the obscurity of authorial intention, an issue raised in both the original version of *You Shall Know Our Velocity* and even more directly in *A Heartbreaking Work of Staggering Genius*. Finally, Hand's interpretation directly affirms important aspects of Will's perspective. Hand insists on both the sincerity and the ridiculousness of their trip, outlining a series of "absurdities" that underlie their journey: "It's absurd, I think, that humans can travel around the world in a matter of days. It's absurd that some have the funds . . . to do so, while thousands go without necessities every day. It's ridiculous that we still would go on such a trip, thinking it justifiable that if we gave back along the way, all would be somehow rectified. And of course it's without logic or any sense of rightness that Will and I would be in a position to do this, given our unremarkableness in so many ways" (275).

Hand also reinforces one central aspect of Will's developmental arc. In a discussion of his own love of information, Hand claims to have believed, "as a younger man, that the things I knew and would know were bricks in something that would, effortlessly, eventually, shape into something recognizable, meaningful. . . . But here I am now, so many years on, and if there is a shape to all this, it hasn't revealed itself . . . what might connect all these things, connective tissue or synapses, or just some sense of order, doesn't exist" (276). Hand agrees, however, that the threat of randomness and incoherence should never stop people from trying. His "Interruption" builds toward a forceful call to action that champions blundering but goodhearted efforts to "weave communion between people" over "stasis" and "criminal" inaction (298).

CHAPTER 4

What Is the What

Dave Eggers's third major work, *What Is the What,*[1] tells the life story of Valentino Achak Deng, a Sudanese "Lost Boy" who collaborated on the project with Eggers. Deng lived with his family in Marial Bai, a small village in southern Sudan, until the outbreak of what has come to be called the Second Sudanese Civil War, a conflict between the central government and the Sudan People's Liberation Army (SPLA). The war, which lasted from the early 1980s through the signing of a comprehensive peace agreement in 2005, is often described in binary terms, with the central government representing the north, its Arab inhabitants, or a form of Islamic fundamentalism practiced by some in the region. In contrast, the SPLA is generally associated with the south, the country's African peoples, or Christianity.

When a militia invaded Marial Bai, Deng, who was no more than six or seven years old at the time, hid in the wall of a local church and watched as men burned the town, killed his neighbors, and rounded up women and children. In Eggers's account, Deng fled into the woods, where he wandered until he met up with a group of young boys on their way east. After walking hundreds of miles through war-torn lands with little food or water, the so-called Lost Boys crossed the border into Ethiopia and settled in what would become a large refugee camp. Deng spent three years at Pinyudo before political instability in Ethiopia forced the refugees to flee back to southern Sudan and ultimately to a camp at Kakuma, in northern Kenya.

Along the way, children were eaten by lions and blown up by bombs. Others starved to death or died of unnamed diseases. The camps provided some stability and at least one meal a day, but these makeshift towns were far from ideal. Deng says, "In Kakuma, a small community of tents grew to a vast patchwork of shanties and buildings constructed from poles and sisal bags and mud, and this is where we lived and worked and went to school from 1992 to 2001. It is not the worst place on the continent of Africa, but it is among them" (370–71). Beyond the difficult conditions, these camps were riddled with tensions. Conflicts sprang up between displaced local populations and refugees; soldiers struggled with both the locals and the migrant boys they sought to recruit; and the refugees struggled with one another, often over the limited resources that were available to them. In the camp at Pinyudo, Deng goes down to the river for water and finds the bloated corpse of a soldier who had been stabbed three times (260). Later, when Deng goes for a walk with a local priest, they pass a group of men watching a soldier rape a local woman. Deng notes, "we altered our course" (286).

While suffering is certainly a central element of Deng's childhood, the book is by no means a mere inventory of atrocities. Amid the loss and deprivation, *What* tells a compelling coming-of-age story. Deng goes to school, has his first sexual experiences, falls in love, and begins to take on increasingly important leadership roles at the camp. His difficult circumstances do not become a mere backdrop for this personal growth, but they do not supersede the narrator's story, either. The two elements work together, with the historical information serving in part to contextualize the difficult challenges that the Lost Boys faced. As Deng says early on in the story, "we adapt, all of us, to the most absurd situations" (47).

The account of Deng's childhood approaches its climax when foreign humanitarian groups begin "resettling" the Lost Boys in Western countries. As his excitement about the prospect of coming to the United States builds, Deng says that waiting to be selected for resettlement is like being a bystander at the Rapture: "all those I knew were pulled from our purgatory and lifted up to the Kingdom of God" (490). The parallel may be conventional (hell/war, Kakuma/purgatory, United States/heaven), but it conveys the mindset of these expectant young men. They giddily imagine living lives of ease in a land of abundance. When the instructors at a frantic two-day orientation class compare expected earnings at minimum wage jobs in the United States with the boys' estimated expenses, Deng realizes, "we could not afford to live on $5 or $6 an hour. No particular solution was offered, I don't think, but we were too high to dwell on the details" (514).

The story of Deng's time in Africa concludes the night before his departure. The boys who are travelling must prepare to leave behind everything they know and fly across the ocean. Deng lays awake all night, "electric" with the "great terrible limitless possibility of the morning" (532). This conclusion sets up a narrative arc reminiscent of many traditional (Eurocentric) Western stories. The American literary corpus is littered with tales of deprived immigrants inspired by the opportunities available in the United States. Yet Eggers's text complicates this story by beginning the book five years after Deng has arrived in America, just four months after his Sudanese girlfriend has been stabbed to death by an ex-boyfriend. The story of his childhood is told in flashbacks over a troubled two-day period.

In the first chapter, Deng opens his Atlanta apartment to a woman who claims to have been in an accident. Her partner, a large man with a gun, comes in behind her. After stealing everything of value, the couple leave the apartment with Deng still tied up on the floor. He cannot get free until his roommate, another Sudanese man named Achor Achor, returns home the following afternoon. The two men then wait nearly an hour for a police officer, a woman in "half of a police uniform" who does little more than give them a complaint card (236). Deng receives similar treatment at the emergency room, where he waits more than twelve hours for someone to look at a gash in his head. He leaves in the middle of the night, still untreated, and sits in his car until it is time for work, a 6 A.M. shift at the front desk of a health club.

All of the time Deng spends waiting over these two days succinctly encapsulates one aspect of his life in the United States. He arrived clinging to the promise of prosperity and planned to begin his new life immediately at a four-year college. Five years later, he has been rejected by schools all around the country and is still taking preparatory classes for an associate's degree at a junior college. One admissions officer, in a moment of striking candor, tells him that he might be too old. When pressed to explain, the officer says, "picture some white suburban family. They're spending forty thousand dollars to send their young blond daughter to college, she's never been away from home, and the first day on campus they see a guy like you roaming the dorms" (473). This narrative strand concludes when Deng leaves work, determined to quit his job and start again somewhere else, a "quieter place" where he can reflect on his life and "make some new plans" (533).

Both stories are intertwined throughout the book, as Deng's past is revealed through flashbacks that occur as he waits for things to happen in the present. This structure allows each narrative to inform the other as both stories unfold simultaneously. Deng's growing hope for the promise of America is colored by the reader's knowledge of the very different kinds of hardships he will face once he arrives. Yet again, neither side of the dichotomy entirely supersedes the other. Deng's willingness to persevere in the face of his challenges in the United States and the continued opportunities that his host country affords him prevent his hardships from cynically cancelling out the sense of hope that comes with his impending trip to the United States. However, that hope is certainly qualified by the realities that Deng faces when he comes to Atlanta. As in Eggers's earlier work, progress, if that term is useful at all in this context, is circuitous and often provisional.

The difficulty of advancement is literal in the early parts of the narrative, when the line of boys meanders through the Sudanese countryside. They often scatter in the face of threats and are forced to regroup and cover the same ground over again. At other times, they simply get turned around and wind up moving in a circle. In America, progress is a more complicated issue. While considering the places he could go in America, for instance, Deng mentions that many Sudanese move to the Great Plains because it is relatively inexpensive to live there and there are high-paying jobs in the meat-processing industry. He notes that men "are paid to divide and carve the animals, cattle, that in many parts of our native Sudan were only to be slaughtered as sacrifices on the most sacred of occasions. . . . The Sudanese in American have become butchers" (27). The loss of spirituality and respect for animals is given a negative cast here, and the loaded term "butcher," used in the context of the atrocities committed against people in southern Sudan, suggests his disapproval. Later in the text, he will remember his father making similar comments in a disparaging description of the northern Arabs: "They were very bad herdsmen, the Arabs were, and because they didn't understand the value of cattle, they only butchered them. They were confused people, my father often told me, hopeless in many ways" (63).

Deng often resists such stereotyping, just as he refuses to openly disparage those who choose to make money by carving up animals. Yet he remains clearly conflicted throughout the text. At the first mention of the practice, he ambivalently concludes, "I am unsure whether this is a giant leap forward" (27). The term "giant leap" recalls the wild hopes that the Sudanese had before coming to America, hopes that hardly seem fulfilled by such a mean existence. Yet it leaves open the possibility that the move does reflect some form of progress. Deng repeatedly praises the opportunities and conveniences that America affords him, and he approves of some changes in traditional customs. While working with a drama club in Kakuma, for example, he and other children write plays that champion gender equality and question Sudanese practices, such as forced marriage (415–16). At the same time, in America, he worries about the men's literal and metaphorical distance from life in southern Sudan. One man, Deng says, returned home for a visit and was sick for a week after drinking the water. Again, Deng points out that the incident might be a bad sign, but he resists making an unequivocal judgment: "We have been weakened by our time in America, perhaps" (506). Deng's uncertainties, much like the bifurcated narrative structure, complicate simplistic linear readings of the text. From his limited perspective within the events being described, the way forward is never clear, and every choice has its costs as well as its potential benefits.

His struggle to understand the direction of events is complicated by the chaotic and seemingly illogical actions that surround him. In Sudan, as the boys, malnourished and nearly naked, stumble across the land, a giant bomber doubles back to hurl explosives in their direction. Later on, a trio of low-flying helicopters that could easily have targeted the boys instead ignores them. Deng concludes, "We never could understand the philosophy of the Sudanese army. Sometimes we were worth their bullets and bombs, and other times we were not" (211). Deng's efforts to understand often give way to bewilderment, from the first attacks on his village ("I had no idea what was happening anymore" [85]) through his resettlement in America ("None of it made sense. It was logical, much more so, that the whole affair would be called off" [517]) to all of the unpredictable events that follow.

The confusion generated by the war only makes matters worse, especially in a country with poorly distributed technology. Concrete information is scarce, and news often travels by word of mouth. Even the military has a limited ability to keep track of people and actions in the war. As the boys wander, they run across confused and isolated bands of soldiers, and Deng's childhood friend Moses is imprisoned after he enlists because soldiers confuse him with another person named Moses. He is forced to stand upright in a livestock pen for two days, with only a two-hour break for sleeping at dawn, before the mistake is corrected (376).

Beyond a generic statement about the general unpredictability of the universe and the chaos generated by war, Eggers's text strongly emphasizes the limited perspective of its protagonist. As a boy in the war, he stumbles through incidents that he understands in only the vaguest way. Deng is six or seven when his village is first attacked, for reasons that he can hardly fathom, and he is forced to flee alone, without any direction or possible destination. Dut Majok, a young teacher who leads the boys' march across southern Sudan to Pinyudo, attempts to explain the war to Deng and one of his friends. The boys must continually interrupt his story because they have very little experience with anything outside their village. When Dut Majok mentions that Ethiopia is another country very similar to Sudan, Deng's friend asks, "If it's like us, why is it somewhere else?" (131).

Even more striking than the boys' uncertainty about *where* they are going is the looming question of *why* they are being led. The soldiers that they encounter along the way refer to them as "Red Army," and some know Dut Majok. His motives are not questioned by the young Deng, but one reviewer, Thomas Jones, raises the obvious questions that face readers: "is he leading the boys to safety, or into recruitment into the SPLA? Is one a condition for the other?"[2] Motivation remains a complex issue throughout the book, long after Deng has learned enough to begin seeing the "architecture" behind local events (318). He is often harassed by those who might be expected to help (the SPLA, other southern Sudanese people), and he finds help in the most random places.

Deng's confusion is compounded when he travels to another culture with almost no knowledge of its traditions or customs. In one telling moment, he carefully compiles his important official documents before coming to America, a file that includes "proof of completion of a course in refereeing, my CPR certification, my drama-group membership card" (517). The book begins with Deng opening his door to the woman who will rob him, and it is a powerful symbolic statement that his door has no peephole. In this country, Deng generalizes, "Our peripheral vision is poor. . . . In the U.S., we do not see trouble coming" (236).

In response to this sense of chaos and disorder, Deng carefully notes the hierarchies and structures that emerge around him, and he takes comfort in organizational details. After a sponsor's daughter shows Deng how to put birthdays into his telephone, he begins entering the dates for everyone he meets. The act provides "a pleasure born of some sense of order" (115). Similarly, the book is haunted by Deng's dream of a final resting place, the Rapturous ascent to heaven noted earlier.

Yet it is not simply the promise of America that pulls Deng through the text. For much of his childhood, he is largely unaware of the outside world. It is his powerful and adaptive sense of hope, which wavers before some of the horrors in the text but never completely disappears, that allows him to keep going. On the long trek through the desert, Deng watches countless children die, and many others lose their minds from all manner of deprivations. He buries one of his childhood friends with his bare hands. Still, he fantasizes about a place where there would be "plenty of meat, and nuts and stew. There would be clean water where we could bathe, and there would be wells for each home, each full of cool water to drink. . . . I would have a new family in Ethiopia, with a mother and father who would bring me close and call me son" (214).

Deng's hopes, however, are repeatedly undermined by the realities that he encounters. The boys cross a river that divides Sudan and Ethiopia, only to find a field full of sick and dying refugees. Deng spends the next few days muttering the phrase that could serve as a mantra for his journey: "this is not that place" (227). Things do not improve much at the string of refugee camps after Pinyudo, and, as noted, America could never live up to the unrealistic hopes of the refugees. The southern Sudanese people and the SPLA, those supposed saviors who never seem to be around when northern forces arrive, also repeatedly fail to live up to young Deng's hopeful expectations.

Despite this pattern, the book as a whole does not simply promote a hardened realism. Fantasies, symbols, and visions play a key role throughout the text and help Deng stay alive. He ruminates on the power of fantasy early in the text, after awakening from a dream in which he is curled up with his mother: "How strange that a dream could make you warm when your body knew exactly how cold it was" (146). During the long walk to safety, his fantastic visions of Ethiopia and other destinations often keep him walking when his strength or health begins to fail. Deng also cultivates the memory of an "ideal day," a pastiche of his happiest childhood moments, and uses it to focus his mind on the long walks (33).

Beyond the personal sphere, Deng places hope in the power of symbolic moments to focus public attention and perhaps even incite action. The book itself could be said to function in this way, as an individual story that could potentially galvanize support for people in southern Sudan. In the preface, Deng says he wants this book "to reach out to others to help them understand Sudan's place in our global community . . . we can make a difference" (xiv–xv). In the narrative itself, the fictionalized Deng calls attention to the larger potential of symbols through the story of the yacht of the Sudanese president, Omar al-Bashir. When members of the African Union were to visit al-Bashir in Khartoum, he imported a $4.5-million yacht, replete with satellite TVs, fine china, and lavish staterooms, from Slovenia to sail the dignitaries up and down the Nile. However, the 172-ton boat had to be towed to the capital first. According to Deng, the boat "challenged" bridges and required 132 sets of overhead electrical wires to be taken down so that the boat could pass. The whole process took so long that it arrived well after the meeting had taken place. Deng notes, "before the boat reached Khartoum, it had become a symbol for how decadent and callous Bashir is." He hopes that this powerful emblem can motivate people in a way that the steady trickle of news stories about genocide and unchecked violence has not (469–70).

Conversely, Deng's darkest moment in Africa comes when he gives up his illusions. On the final stretch of his walk into Kakuma, he explicitly compares this trip with the boys' earlier arrival in Ethiopia. The juxtaposition highlights his current, more realistic perspective: "I remembered my thoughts about buildings and waterfalls in Ethiopia, and my disappointment when, after crossing the border, I found only more of the blight we thought we had left. . . . Kenya's leadership could turn over just as Ethiopia's had, and there would be another [massacre of refugees]. . . . That night I stopped walking"

(360). Ironically, Deng has lost his eyesight at the end of the walk because of an unidentified illness. As he gives up his illusions, he literally loses the ability to look at the world around him and decides that the best course of action is simply to lay down and die.

These examples suggest the power that the imagination has to recast the world. They also demonstrate the poverty of mere acceptance, a major theme throughout the text. As Deng talks in the present, he directs his flashbacks at those around him who are unsympathetic or just plain oblivious to his plight, whether it be the people robbing his apartment, the employees who cannot help him at the hospital, or the hurried businesspeople passing by his desk at the health club. The Western reader who might know little more about Sudan than the information presented in sound bites is certainly implicated in this process.

Deng himself undergoes a similar transformation in the text. As a child, he hears his father tell the origin story of their people. After God created the earth, he gave the Dinka people a choice. They could have cattle, which would bring them "milk and meat and prosperity of every kind," or they could have the What, an unspecified alternative (62). Deng learns that the Dinka's decision to take the cattle is a reflection of his people's wisdom. The man was able to "take pleasure in the bounty before him, rather than trade it for the unknown. And because the first man was able to see this, God has allowed us to prosper" (62–63). Throughout the novel, Deng wonders what "the what" was, as he searches for a concrete alternative to the traditional path of his people. By the end of the book, he is able to embrace the unknown, and he reverses his original perspective on the story. On the night before he leaves for the United States, he says that his people's choice was an error of "timidity, of choosing what was before us over what might be." As a result, the Dinka had been "punished for centuries" (531). The refugees, however, have chosen a new path. They leap into the unknown, into a new life on a different continent, and this act, Deng asserts, marks a turning point for the Dinka.

Deng's embrace of the unknown is paired in the text with his acceptance of ongoing struggle. His difficulties will not simply end with the discovery of a bountiful Ethiopia or a prosperous United States. A Somali, called the Lost Man in the text, approaches the refugees shortly before they leave Africa and prophetically yells, "It'll be no better. . . . You thought you'd have no problems [elsewhere]? Just different problems, stupid boys!" (528). The boys, of course, are too excited about the journey to pay any attention to this man's ranting, and Deng even notes the larger irony: "this is what was strange about the Lost Man: he was going to America, too" (529). In this regard, *What* seems close to the sensibility that drives *A Heartbreaking Work of Staggering Genius.* Deng's hopeful fantasies drive him forward into the unknown, but his experience shows him that reality will never fully conform to his dreams. He can, in other words, continue to fantasize, but only with an awareness of the fantastic nature of his visions. This tension is, again, enacted in the bifurcated structure of the story, which allows the novel to build toward the great promise of America while simultaneously undercutting, without entirely erasing, that very promise.

The real-life Deng provides the most triumphant acceptance of such tensions in the preface: "This book is a form of struggle, and it keeps my spirit alive to struggle" (xiv). In contrast, the fictionalized Deng often longs for the stability that has vanished from his life and wrestles with the impulse to assert himself. This difficulty is, in part, a reflection of his self-effacing personality. Deng refers to himself at various points in the text as an insect and regularly acknowledges many of his shortcomings. He also notes, with some reservations, his "eagerness to please authority," a trait that "got me into far too much trouble" (465).

Such impulses have also been exacerbated by his chaotic circumstances. Deng is hypervigilant about any action that could get him noticed and reflexively considers worst-case scenarios. As Deng and his friend Achor Achor flee enemy soldiers, they pass a six-month-old baby wailing next to its dead mother. Deng wants to leave it for fear that it will make noise and draw attention to them. He experiences a similar fear in the United States, aggravated in part by the Sudanese boys' limited understanding of the culture. When going to meet a new sponsor, Phil Mays, Deng worries that Mays might be an undercover immigration official. Later, Mays asks Deng and Achor Achor about Sudanese proverbs. Before replying, the two duck into the bathroom to consider the best response. Both fear that the wrong answer could cause Mays to withdraw his assistance. Deng insists "that we all believed, all of us Sudanese, that anything could happen, at any time. . . . I was grateful for any hour in which I was welcomed and not in danger" (171).

The text of *What* itself stands as evidence of Deng's gradual transformation from scared child into a highly visible representative of the Lost Boys. Along the way, many people and events influence his development. Perhaps most prominent, Deng works with a series of teachers and teacher-figures who insistently promote the value of education. From Dut Majok, the young man who leads the boys to Ethiopia, to Gop Chol, with whom Deng lives in Kakuma, the most prominent adults in Deng's life insist that the children need to learn as much as possible so that they will be prepared to lead the new Sudan. His first teacher at Pinyudo, Mr. Kondit, says, "Education will be your mother. Education will be your father. While your older brothers fight this war with guns, when the bullets stop, you will fight the next war with your pens" (297). At the time, the children laugh at the idea of having education for parents, and Deng first excels at school only to impress Mr. Kondit's four beautiful nieces, known throughout the camp as the Royal Girls. However, he continues to work at his studies and is further influenced by the values of the "progressive-minded international consortium" responsible for the camp at Kakuma (441).

Many of Deng's teachers notice his abilities and encourage him to take on larger roles in the classroom and community. Father Matong, the Catholic priest who baptized Deng, even predicts that Deng will one day be an important voice for his people. Matong named him Valentino after a saint who was imprisoned for teaching others about his religion. Valentino converted his jailer's blind daughter and was finally beheaded after she miraculously regained her sight. Matong tells Deng, "I think you will have the power to make people see . . . you will remember what it was like to be here, you will see the lessons here. And someday you will find your own jailer's daughter, and to her you will bring light" (287).

Despite the fact that the book stands as evidence of Father Matong's vision, Deng resists the pressure to be a guiding voice and modestly notes, "Most prophecies go unfulfilled" (288). He does, however, develop a strong sense of responsibility and begins to take on larger roles. In classes at Pinyudo, Mr. Kondit enlists him to take attendance. By the time he reaches Kakuma, Deng is ready to become an official youth leader and then an employee at a new Youth and Culture Program sponsored by a Japanese non-profit company. He oversees events, organizes trips, and mediates disputes between parents and children. By the time the Lost Boys travel to the United States, many are turning to Deng as a de facto leader and source of information. Shortly after arriving, he has to restrict phone calls because his cell is ringing seventy times a day.

Deng's growth as a leader is severely tested in the United States by the relative indifference of most people to the Lost Boys' situation. The text as a whole is structured as a series of internal monologues directed at all those people who seem oblivious to his struggles, and many of those who do acknowledge him do so only in the most general or stereotypical ways. Some are reminded of snippets from the news about Darfur. Others treat him as a generic African; some people call him a "Nigerian," and an African American robber claims that they are "brothers" (5).

While the book as a whole does critique the callousness and apathy that surround Deng, he is quick to point out his own shortcomings. Before he even finds a job in America, Deng and his friends yell "go to work" at homeless people in Atlanta, even though they too are living off of the generosity of others. In addition, the opening pages show how Deng's sympathies change with his situation. When the robbers cannot get the television, they leave a boy of "no more than ten" behind to keep an eye on the apartment until they return (25). Deng is tied up on the floor. At points, he acknowledges that this boy is also a victim of the robbers, and he fantasizes about saving this child from what must be a terrible situation at home. Deng's sympathies, however, quickly vanish at other moments, particularly when the boy refuses to acknowledge Deng's own humanity. At one point, for instance, the boy silences Deng by dropping a phone book on his head, as if he were a bug.

By acknowledging his own limitations, Deng is able to extend sympathy even to those who have wronged him, and he tries throughout the text to acknowledge the complex circumstances the each individual faces. As noted earlier, many Sudanese have taken jobs in the Midwest with meat-processing companies. Deng finds this work distasteful, but he resists the urge to condemn either the practice or the men who participate in it. When Deng considers possibilities for the future at the end of the text, he does clearly assert, "I will not file fabric samples again. I will not haul television sets or sweep tinsel from the floors of a Christmas-themed shop. I will not butcher animals in Nebraska or Kansas." However, he mitigates the implicit judgment of others by quickly adding, "I have no prejudice against these jobs. I have done most of them" (535). For Deng, such life choices are never simple, and he strives to understand others' perspectives even when he clearly wants to distance himself from them.

Eggers takes a slightly different approach in this book than he did in some of his early work. If *A Heartbreaking Work of Staggering Genius,* for instance, is in many ways a bipolar book, *What* resists oversimplifying situations with binary logic, and it rigorously qualifies most of its conclusions. In moments of anger or frustration, Deng often makes rash remarks, as when he flees the attack on his hometown while fulminating about the "Dinka with their useless spears" (106). However, such moments stand out in the story precisely because they conflict with his cautious manner. When another Sudanese man makes a scene at a public event, Deng does not judge his character or attempt to generalize about all Sudanese men in America. He quietly asserts, "I had a very low opinion of this man on this night" (166).

Similarly, Deng is willing to address the complexities of the war, even as he advocates for the rights of southern Sudanese people. The SPLA, whose aims Deng generally supports, rarely appears as a positive force in the book. Recruitment seems like a vaguely menacing prospect. (Those who join up are rarely seen again.) Stories circulate about the harsh treatment of recruits, some of whom are worked to death. Individual soldiers often act with arrogance and impunity in the name of "the cause." Even much later, when the leader of the SPLA, John Garang, attends a meeting in the United States and speaks to the Lost Boys, Deng describes him as "the man who more or less began the civil war that brought war to our homes, the war that brought deaths to our relatives, and set in motion our journey to Ethiopia and later to Kenya" (182). As the war approaches its end, Deng still cannot acknowledge the advances without recalling the costs: "There is pride [in southern Sudan] now, and all the doubts we've had about the SPLA, and all the suffering they caused, have been largely forgiven. If the south achieves freedom it is through their work, however muddled" (49).

Deng takes an equally critical approach to his own attitudes and behaviors, regularly mixing pointed commentary about others with admissions of personal shortcomings. The Lost Boys, he points out, often crafted their stories for Western audiences that expected to be shocked. His own story, however, "includes enough small embellishments that [he] cannot criticize the accounts of others" (21). These admissions create the impression of a thoughtful and sensitive narrator who is, like Eggers's earlier protagonists, profoundly aware of his own limitations. They also allow him to communicate genuine sympathy, even for those who do not seem to merit it.

His own attitude mirrors or at least strives to mirror, that of Amath, a beautiful girl from his village. During the ideal childhood day he recounts early in the text, Deng talks about running down to the river to fetch water for her. Upon returning, he falls face first into the dust. Yet Amath does not laugh or criticize him. Instead, she dusts him off and thanks him for running so fast. Deng praises her ability to notice the best things about him without belittling his faults (45). The story is told through the eyes of an adoring boy as part of a day that has been explicitly constructed, but Amath's sympathetic kindness serves as an ideal that hangs over the text. Later, Deng travels to Nairobi with his drama troupe. While there, his sponsor's girlfriend, Grace, is brought to tears by the news of Princess Diana's death. This surprising display of sympathy is appealing to Deng, and he envisions a world where every death around the globe is reported and collectively mourned.

The desire for genuine community remains with Deng, even as he acknowledges the difficulty, if not the impossibility, of attaining it. Despite all of the horrors that the real Deng has seen, he optimistically claims in the preface that the work was "born out of my faith and beliefs in humanity" (xiv). His fictionalized counterpart shares a similar optimism and repeatedly points out both the unexpected kindnesses he encounters on his travels and the important role that others play while he is on his journey. At several crucial points, he finds his faith shaken or his strength fading and is revived by the presence of others, as when his old childhood friend William K miraculously appears after his closest companion dies. Deng says, "I was so thankful. I felt it was God giving me this gift of William K after taking away [my friend]. . . . It seemed impossible that I would find him here, along the Nile" (187).

Similarly, Deng describes what he calls his "dark days" at the end of the walk to Kakuma (360). After two previous refugee camps, at Pinyudo and Golkur, disbanded in as many years, the trip to Kakuma lacks the periodic bursts of hope and optimism that marked the first walk. Now, Deng says, "there were no promises" (360). To make matters worse, Achor Achor, with whom Deng had been travelling since Pinyudo, has to be taken to a hospital tent for dehydration. Expecting his friend to die, Deng returns to the road, alone and distraught, with his infected eyes nearly swollen shut. Exhaustion quickly overtakes him, and, as the sun falls, Deng lays down in the road, bluntly noting that it is "a good time to die" (360). Again, it takes the intervention of another person to keep him moving: a young girl named Maria badgers him until he gets back up again. Deng, commenting from the present tense of the book, even notes that "had [Achor Achor] and I been together then I might not have fallen so low" (360).

These random moments of outreach and connection help to explain Deng's resilient faith in humanity. The displays of individual weakness also underscore the text's emphasis on community. The Lost Boys are young, malnourished, and uninformed about the conflict taking place all around them. It is only by banding together that most stand any chance of survival. Early on in the trip, the boys fantasize about running back home or finding guns with which to retaliate, but their leader, Dut Majok, sternly reminds them that "for now we're safe in our numbers. Our numbers are our weapon" (119). Their interdependence is symbolically suggested by circular sleeping patterns. Deng's friend Moses tells him of sleeping in a barn full of rats. The boys slept in a circle, with those on the outside remaining awake to scare off the vermin. Deng has a similar experience when his line is attacked by a lion. After several boys are carried off, the rest are afraid to sleep with their back to the grasses, so they too lie in a circle.

From a more practical perspective, organization is also necessary for communities to function. Before Pinyudo is organized, refugees search for food individually. Deng tries to catch fish in a river with a twisted stick and some wire. "When order came to the camp," he says, "life improved" (259). Refugees are placed into groups and chores and distributed throughout the community. For the fictional and the real-life Deng, this form of action has a strong appeal, a belief that is, again, stated most directly in the preface: "Since you and I exist, together we can make a difference" (xv).

Yet, in typical Eggers fashion, the book's acknowledgment of individual vulnerability and weakness does not lead to the wholesale embrace of collective action. Community is, in the first instance, difficult to establish among a group of competing individuals. Even the circle formation that is meant to protect the boys from predators becomes a mobile and thus tenuous form of collectivity, as boys struggle to get away from the edges of the group. Deng falls asleep in the center but wakes up "cold, connected to no one. I looked around only to find the circle had . . . migrated twenty feet to my left, leaving me outside and alone" (32).

Moreover, communities do not organize along equitable lines, if such lines could even be said to exist. Instead, hierarchies form that seem to inevitably benefit some at the expense of others. When Deng hears of a group of boys riding through the desert after them with a water tanker, he muses that this tanker "symbolized for us everything that we would never have, and the fact that there would be, always, castes within castes, that within groups of walking boys, still there were hierarchies" (21). At Pinyudo, the SPLA brings in a commander with expertise in agricultural techniques to help farm the land. Deng notes, "we thought this was a fine idea, but of course we knew that the most difficult aspects of working the land would be left to the unaccompanied minors, and indeed they were" (324). Not only does this commander refuse to use Deng's name, a symbolic gesture that suggests the suppression of Deng's individuality, but he seems unable to recognize the boys as anything but developing soldiers. He views all of their activity from the perspective of the larger collective, leading Deng to wryly comment that "the sight of these emaciated boys working under the summer sun gave him much pleasure" (325).

These communities also have a tendency to generate increasingly intricate systems of rules. As aid workers pour into the camp at Pinyudo, schedules become stricter and activities more regulated. The boys are not allowed to speak to any non-Sudanese person, and they have to deny any knowledge of the SPLA. In the United States, Deng feels completely lost in the elaborate bureaucracies that surround him. After spending hours in a seemingly empty emergency room, he approaches the receptionist, only to have her scurry away from the desk. "We are no longer considered patients here," he bemoans. "No one knows what to do with us. We are furniture" (290).

As noted earlier, Deng feels particularly susceptible to the dictates of authority. His girlfriend, Tabitha, however, encourages him to resist these rules and to embrace individual freedom. She delivers one of the text's major speeches on the subject after he refuses to abandon the camp and build a new life with her in Nairobi: "You're a soul whose human form happened to take that of a boy from Sudan. But you're not tied to that. . . . What right do all these people have to draw boundaries around the life you can live? What gives them the right?" (464). At the time, Deng sees this perspective as "irresponsible and shortsighted and immature," but Deng the narrator, who is radically reassessing his life after Tabitha's death, interjects (465). From the textual present, the "wisdom" in her speech is more apparent to him, and he laments his "lack of urgency" (353).

Eggers introduces similar complexities in *A Heartbreaking Work of Staggering Genius,* as the narrator struggles with the conflict between his desire to create and the historical conditions that constrain every act of creation. While the general conflict between an individual will and historically entrenched structures is depicted in both books, Eggers develops the problem further in *What* by explicitly situating his characters within larger sociopolitical systems. The text as a whole is attentive to the ways in which these systems channel and constrain individual actions, even as it acknowledges the malleability of the structures themselves. Deng, for instance, complains about the bureaucratic processes that fail to recognize his individuality, and it is the imprecision of such mechanisms that, say, allow his friend Moses to be imprisoned at the SPLA training grounds for the crimes of another person named Moses. It is, however, the very imprecision of these systems that affords Deng some freedom to operate. At Kakuma, Deng leaves the camp without identification, hoping to return and be reprocessed as a different person. This practice, colloquially referred to as "recycling," allows individuals to acquire multiple ration cards. As he walks out of town, Deng muses, "I was off into the night, with no identifying papers on me. I was new, I was no one" (396).

At some points in the text, the ability to manipulate the system is figured as empowering, a way for those who have few opportunities to make some small advances. After universities repeatedly dismiss his applications, Deng refuses to become discouraged. Instead, he stresses the need for more "creativity" and reminisces, "At Kakuma we could invent a new name for ourselves, a new story for whatever purpose, whenever the pressures and obligations necessitated it . . . there were few unbendable rules" (473). Similarly, he discusses the way that boys craft their stories when applying to the United Nations for resettlement in the United States. The boys have to write autobiographical statements, and they quickly develop guidelines. One needs to emphasize ongoing persecution in Kakuma or Sudan so that there is a strong justification for relocation. One should not have living parents. One should never mention involvement with the SPLA.

Despite the advantages to be won by gaming the system, Deng feels uncomfortable with the process. He resists lying in his own autobiographical statement to the UN and worries about "whether or not this picture, these words, were truly me" (486). During an interview, the representative from the UN seems surprised to hear Deng admit that his parents are not dead. Yet, even as he fights to maintain his identity, Deng does manipulate the system, and he struggles to accept that his identity can be clearly or easily represented. In a passage that echoes Eggers's narrator in *A Heartbreaking Work of Staggering Genius,* Deng says, "How could I put everything down on paper? It seemed impossible. No matter what, the majority of life would be left out of this story, this sliver of a version of the life I'd known" (485). Given such a perspective, it is not surprising that the title page lists both a subtitle, "The Autobiography of Valentino Achak Deng," and the seemingly contradictory generic classification "A Novel." Even an MRI feels like a "violation" to Deng, who complains about strangers having access to pictures of his brain without truly knowing anything about him (315).

These conflicts over truth and representation are not limited to discussions of identity in the text. They appear just as frequently in commentary on the power of narrative more generally. Deng, for instance, notes the ways in which stories by and about the Lost Boys are manipulated for specific audiences or to achieve particular effects. At Pinyudo, the SPLA considers the boys "aid bait" and bars them from speaking with any of the aid workers (326). The media in the United States, in contrast, want shocking stories and become accustomed to certain striking elements in Sudanese accounts. As a result, "the tales of the Lost Boys have become remarkably similar over the years" (21).

The book as a whole participates in this process by using an accessible human story to frame the larger crisis in Sudan. By creating a coherent linear narrative with a strong emotional appeal, the novel confronts both Western indifference and the complex accounts that emerge through the Sudanese government's propaganda, Western media, and the many individual stories that begin to circulate shortly after resettlement begins. When the SPLA splits into two rebel factions, Deng laments the time and lives lost to infighting, but he also notes the narrative challenge that the split represents. For those unfamiliar with the country, the clear binary account (north/south, Arab/Christian, good/evil) is lost, allowing "the world to turn an indifferent eye to the decimation of Sudan: the civil war became, to the world at large, too confusing to decipher, a mess of tribal conflicts with no clear heroes and villains" (349).

Deng, as noted, tends to emphasize the particularities of any individual situation, and he does not try to oversimplify the conflict. However, he also resists the idea that the situation is somehow too complex or provincial for outsiders, a position often strategically promoted by the government to derail Western interference. For all of the uncertainties and ambiguities that arise throughout the text, Eggers periodically interrupts the narrative to present a history of the conflict in Sudan, from British and Egyptian intervention in the nineteenth century through the comprehensive peace agreement in 2005. These informational interjections are often staged as lectures from Deng's teachers.

Given the text's emphasis on the individual and its insistence on the inherently political dimension of narrative (every story is a necessarily incomplete version of events told for a particular purpose), one might expect any such narrative to come under direct scrutiny. This selective history certainly elides some facts and perspectives in its presentation of a worldview that largely accords with Deng's local experiences. Yet these lectures remain largely unchallenged in the narrative and are even used to counter alternative accounts of events. Shortly after fleeing Marial Bai, Deng meets an old Dinka man who explains that the attacks are a punishment from God, who is exacting punishment for some uncertain transgression through "lion-people . . . . Arabs who have fallen to the level of the animal" (99). Despite the text's willingness to allow for individual perspectives, this position is explicitly dismissed when Dut Majok explains the current state of the conflict (129–30). There are certainly some ways in which his authoritative account could be qualified. Deng, for instance, notes that such accounts are generally constructed after the fact and are distinct from the chaotic and unpredictable experience of living in history. From a local perspective, the path is not clear and the outcomes are uncertain. Still, the text on the whole moves much closer than Eggers's early work to the acceptance of an authoritative history, or it is at least more willing to present a history as authoritative in the service of transcending apathy and indifference.

This perspective also fits with the text's respect for teacher figures and Deng's own gradual development in Western-influenced educational settings. He appreciates the usefulness of rationality and learns to value formal education. (His primary ambition in the United States seems to be to attend a four-year university.) Again, Eggers's earlier work would have been much more likely to make the potential contradictions in these views explicit. Many discussions of *A Heartbreaking Work of Staggering Genius* remain mired in the work's metafictional trappings and never get past pseudophilosophical debates about the possibility of conveying truth in fiction, the role of rationality in an unpredictable universe, or the conflict between limited individual perspectives and a transcendent (and perhaps fictional) view of history. While all of these elements certainly appear in *What,* the logical and literary gamesmanship of the early work remains secondary to the narrative account of Deng's life. As a result, the novel can convey Deng's chaotic and limited impressions along with his growing awareness of historical forces and, to use Deng's phrase, the "architecture of it all" (318). It is a book that works through individual experience but reaches for larger truths. In an essay on the construction of the book, Eggers admits his desire to have the work "transcend the many human rights reports and newspapers articles already available to the world."[3] At the same time, both he and Deng readily acknowledge that it is finally the story of one man. Deng, being interviewed along with Eggers, emphatically states, "This is my story and not the story of the thousands of Lost Boys in America. There are many experiences in the story that we all shared. . . . But my life is different in many ways. This is a story of my life, not everyone's life. We are all different people."[4]

By sharing his story, Deng is reaching out to others with an optimism and a faith in humanity that are difficult to fathom in the face of the novel's events. The conclusion itself is not wholly optimistic. Deng is resigned to continue struggling with the traumas that seem to follow him wherever he goes, and he still seems burdened by the intense pressures that come with the Sudanese boys to America. They arrive with unrealistic expectations for the future and a desire to make the Sudanese people proud. They also carry the hope of all those left behind. Even as the boys struggle to survive on minimum-wage jobs in the United States, some of their friends and relatives still imagine them as wealthy benefactors who should be able to send money back to Africa. In the present moment of the novel, Deng is wearied by the supposed promises of America and laments that "too many have fallen, too many feel they have failed. The pressures upon us, the promises we cannot keep with ourselves—these things are making monsters of too many of us" (8).

Yet, at the end of the story, Deng still has options. There are people around the country who would happily help him, and there are places that he can go to rest and reflect on recent events. Despite the dark moments after Tab's death, when he briefly "lived without God," Deng also maintains his religious faith, one last crucial element of the text worth mentioning. Eggers does suggest that Deng's Christianity is the product of foreign influence and presents alternative perspectives on faith in Sudan. Many in Marial Bai ascribe to various forms of Christianity. Deng was converted by his Uncle Jok at a very young age. Yet Deng's own father maintains ties to traditional belief systems and offers multiple justifications for his choice. Beyond faith, he prefers polygamy to monogamy and, being illiterate, is skeptical of Christianity's reliance on written words. He derides it as a "Church of Books" (13).

This kind of contextualization, however, is ultimately overshadowed by Deng's meditations on faith. The death, misery, and violence that surround him make his insistent belief in God all the more impressive. He maintains this faith, in part, through a deistic vision of the universe, wherein God does not intervene in human affairs. After Tab's death, he presses this point further: "God is in my life but I do not depend on him. My God is not a reliable God" (358). The use of "my" here, implying a version of God that belongs specifically to Deng, fits with his insistence on the particularity of individual experience, just as his willingness to reconsider his relation to God confirms his reflective tendencies. Throughout the text, he puzzles over the signs in his life and vacillates between asking God for help and wondering if he has been targeted for punishment. After Tabitha's death, Deng turns to two texts, *The Purpose-Driven Life* by Rick Warren and *Seeking the Heart of God* by Mother Teresa and Brother Roger, in his effort to reconnect with his faith and find direction. The result is, as might be expected, more ambivalence. At times, Deng says that passages "seem written for me," but, at other moments, the same words feel "hollow and unconvincing" (358–59). All in all, it is a nuanced depiction of a thoughtful man struggling with his beliefs.

The book as a whole builds on Deng's faith and is littered with biblical symbols and references. The woman who saves Deng's life on the road to Kakuma, for instance, is named Maria. The numbers three and twelve also spring up throughout the text, referring back to Catholicism's vision of a triune God and related accounts of the apostles, respectively. These references provide structure by weaving Deng's belief system into the text. From a different perspective, the repetitive use of biblical names serves to remind readers of the real consequences of Western missionary work. The text also adopts familiar structural devices (such as a three-section narrative that revolves in part around death and rebirth) while also referring, albeit somewhat obliquely, to the historical circumstances that produced those devices.

The novel as a whole operates in an equally bifurcated way, moving toward the moment at which Deng abandons his current life even as it documents his growth. If Deng's optimistic speech before leaving Africa has been in some ways challenged by the second narrative strand of the book, it does reflect Deng's development into the kind of man who can stand up and speak his mind despite staggering fears and uncertainties. The text as a whole concludes with Deng in the narrative present and remains equally split. Early in the book, Deng says that the label "Lost Boys," however the refugees might actually feel about it, is quite appropriate, and not merely for its historical reference. The boys were forced out of their villages and did leave their families behind. Yet they are no more settled in the present. Deng questions whether he can appropriately be called Sudanese, given that he lived in Sudan only as a small child and has not been back in two decades. Moreover, his time in the United States makes the prospect of return, at least on any long-term basis, unlikely. As the literary critic Aliki Varvogli puts it, "Deng's education and his life experience in the US have already remade him in ways that are bound to render a return home problematic: he can only return as an outsider, having come of age elsewhere and been made famous by an American book."[5] And yet the United States is never really home for him either.

This lingering sense of uncertainty hangs over the end of the book, and yet, as is evidenced by the book itself, Deng is willing to speak his mind. The concluding paragraph reaches out directly to the reader and calls for collective action. It is a bold assertion of Deng's voice, even if that voice is committed to the inevitability of struggle in a random and often-indecipherable universe. He says, "Whatever I do, however I find a way to live, I will tell these stories. . . . I will tell stories to people who will listen and to people who don't want to listen, to people who seek me out and to those who run. All the while I will know that you are there. How can I pretend that you do not exist? It would be almost as impossible as you pretending that I do not exist" (535).

A Note on the Critical Response: Eggers's first book is an autobiography that uses self-conscious interjections to point out some of the work's most notable fictionalizations. His second book is expressly fiction, but it plays with the fiction/nonfiction divide through inset photos, Hand's counternarrative, and a series of references outside the text that situate both the characters and the novel on a seemingly realistic timeline. The third book foregrounds its autobiographical elements by including a preface written by the real-life counterpart of the book's protagonist, a map of Sudan, and a subtitle that includes the word "autobiography." The book, however, is also classified as a novel, and authorship is clearly attributed to Dave Eggers alone. Eggers and Deng have been forthcoming about the ways in which the story was fictionalized (time was modified for narrative flow, some characters were created or formed as composites of real-life people, representative events from the lives of other refugees were included as part of Deng's story). Both men also insist that, despite these modifications, the book tries to capture Deng's speech patterns along with his experiences. In one interview, Eggers calls it a "fictionalized autobiography in Valentino's voice" and says that it was written while listening to tapes of his conversations with Deng.[6]

Many critics and readers have accepted these explanations, praising the book for both its truthfulness and its emotional force. In a lengthy review of the book, Kevin Brooks advises that readers should not "get hung up on the question of authorship, or become overly concerned about the veracity of the novel. Eggers's collaboration with Deng has been an open, acknowledged collaboration, and the major events of the novel are not fictionalized, only stylized."[7] Other critics, however, have found the issue of authorship a bit more problematic. The most vociferous attack has come from author and cultural critic Lee Siegel in a review written for the *New Republic.* Siegel finds Eggers's fictionalizing presence in and around the text deeply problematic because "life and death are balanced on the difference between truth and falsehood." When the government in Khartoum denies programmatic killing, Siegel asserts, the "most powerful argument against the mass murderers . . . is the testimony of the victims." As a result, he sees Eggers's ownership of the text as a form of "post-colonial arrogance"[8] wherein "Deng's personhood has been displaced by someone else's style and sensibility—by someone else's story."[9]

Just as the metafictional apparatus of *A Heartbreaking Work of Staggering Genius* has dominated critical conversations about that work, the related issues of voice, authorship, and ownership hang over commentary on *What.* These subjects are particularly fraught in the context of American race relations, where relatively privileged whites have long served as the primary public representatives of African American experiences. Yet even the most determined critics of Eggers's text acknowledge the sincere intentions behind it. All of the proceeds from the book go to the Valentino Achak Deng Foundation, which the two established to help improve the lives of Sudanese people in southern Sudan and the United States. In 2009, the Foundation opened up a secondary school in Marial Bai, the first in the region.

CHAPTER 5

Zeitoun

Eggers first met the Zeitouns, the family at the center of his fourth major work, *Zeitoun*,[1] through the Voice of Witness foundation. Eggers cofounded the Voice of Witness, along with Lola Vollen, to collect the stories of people affected by human rights crises around the world. The series has published collections on topics ranging from wrongful incarceration in the United States to the impact of the Sudanese civil war. The Zeitoun family's story was featured in *Voices from the Storm: The People of New Orleans on Hurricane Katrina and Its Aftermath*. According to Eggers's "Notes on Process and Methodology," their story stuck with him, and he arranged to talk with the family on a subsequent trip to New Orleans. The initial meeting began a "three-year process of interviews and research" that culminated in *Zeitoun* (335).

This quick sketch suggests a few significant similarities between *Zeitoun* and Eggers's previous book, *What Is the What*. Both resulted from lengthy engagements with victims of human rights abuses. These engagements led, in both cases, to narrative accounts of the tragedies, told from the perspective of particular protagonists (as opposed to, say, works that attempt to document the tragedies from a more removed, historical perspective). Moreover, Eggers has made claims about the authenticity of both works. As noted in the previous chapter, Eggers says that *What Is the What* attempts to capture the real Valentino Achak Deng's voice and to relate larger truths about the lives of Sudanese refugees. Similarly, the paratextual materials in *Zeitoun* assert that the book is "based primarily on the accounts" of its protagonists, Abdulrahman and Kathy Zeitoun (xv). The narrative "reflects their recollections" (335).

Given these similarities, the difference in *Zeitoun*'s rhetorical positioning is notable. Eggers referred to *What Is the What* as "fictionalized autobiography," a claim that raised many questions about the actual process of composition and the ethics of collaborative authorship. Some critics even noted that Deng's yearning for acknowledgment and connection in the text implicitly positions Eggers as a savior, the invisible figure who has brought this man's story to a wider audience. In contrast, Eggers chose to categorize *Zeitoun* as a work of nonfiction, with multiple references in the paratextual material to fact checking, independent sources, and processes of verification. There are also lengthy sections at the end of the text listing "books and reports [that] were crucial to the writing of *Zeitoun*," the work of relevant "journalists and researchers," and "agencies and organizations [that] provided essential information" (331–34). In interviews and statements about the book, Eggers has repeatedly referred to his undergraduate studies in journalism and has mentioned his experience as a feature writer for *Esquire*.

Similarly, Eggers notes at the beginning of the book that "conversations have been recounted as best as can be remembered by the participants" (xv). In *A Heartbreaking Work of Staggering Genius*, such an admission served in part to foreground the inherent problems in contemporary conceptions of "fiction" and "nonfiction." In *What*, Deng's preface cites his inability to remember childhood conversations as one of the primary reasons for designating the book as a novel. Here, Eggers simply notes the issue, accepting the supposed limitations of his journalistic process, and quickly moves the audience along to the story itself. As if to further solidify his commitment to the true story that is about to unfold, Eggers has also moved a notice about profit distribution, which appeared in the back of *What*, to the front of the book. The profits from *Zeitoun*, the reader is immediately notified, are being donated to a foundation that is "dedicated to rebuilding New Orleans and fostering interfaith understanding" (ix).

If Eggers's new journalistic persona does not necessarily eliminate the ethical and theoretical issues that motivated questions about his authorship of *What*, it does provide him with a more conventional relationship to his subject, one far less likely to inspire questions about his role in the production of the narrative. It also foregrounds truthfulness, an issue that has become increasingly prominent in the years since the book's publication. While little has been said to challenge Eggers's account of events, his depiction of the loving couple is potentially belied by the Zeitouns' subsequent divorce and its nasty follow-up. Abdulrahman has been charged with domestic abuse, which Kathy has testified dates back to the beginning of their marriage, in 1994, and in late 2012 he was indicted for allegedly attacking his ex-wife and then ordering a hit on her while in prison.

These events have brought some back to the very questions about process and authorship that the book's designation as "nonfiction" helped to circumvent. The author Victoria Patterson has questioned the Zeitouns' close involvement in the construction of the novel: "If you had editorial privilege of your own story, would you whitewash? Would you be tempted to be more heroic, smarter, prettier, kinder, funnier, friendlier, and on and on?"[2] Sara Foss ruminates on these comments in her blog for *The Daily Gazette,* wondering, first, how much Eggers knew and, second, how these events should impact her own experience of the book in late 2012.[3] Others have been even more dismissive. Edward Champion, managing editor of the online cultural forum *Reluctant Habits,* called the book a "misleading feel-good hagiography."[4] Adam Martin, being a bit more circumspect in *The Atlantic Wire,* speculates that this already-flawed book will come to seem "much more sinister" if Zeitoun is convicted.[5]

As the tenor of these comments suggest, the debate extends beyond quibbling about the designation of the book. Eggers explores his characters' histories in some detail, and the Zeitouns' relationship is central to the emotional architecture of the work. Moreover, Eggers, in typical fashion, is careful to define the scope of the work in his opening "Notes": "This book does not attempt to be an all-encompassing book about New Orleans or Hurricane Katrina. It is only an account of one family's experiences before and after the storm" (xv). While the narrative is propelled by a compelling sequence of events and provides a distinct historical perspective on the hurricane and its aftermath, the work is deeply invested in the lives of its protagonists and foregrounds their unique histories.

The story centers around the arrest and imprisonment of Abdulrahman Zeitoun in the aftermath of Hurricane Katrina. Zeitoun, born in 1957, is raised in Jableh, Syria, but moves to the United States in 1988. When Hurricane Katrina reaches Louisiana in late August 2005, he is living in New Orleans with his wife, Kathy, their three daughters, and Kathy's son from a previous marriage. Kathy and Zeitoun run a successful contracting company, Zeitoun A. Painting Contractor LLC, and own a handful of properties around the city. As warnings about the approaching storm became more urgent, Kathy takes the children to her brother's house in Baton Rouge. Zeitoun decides to keep an eye on their buildings. When the levees give way and large portions of the city flood, Zeitoun pitches a tent on the roof of his house and uses an old canoe to visit his properties, helping stranded people and animals along the way.

One of his buildings miraculously has both a functioning telephone and running water, so it becomes an informal hub for Zeitoun and several acquaintances who have remained in New Orleans. One afternoon, Zeitoun gets out of the shower and is talking to his brother on the phone when a group of armed people in bulletproof vests, "with mismatched police and military uniforms," burst through the front door (206). They take Zeitoun and three other men to the Union Passenger Terminal, a docking station for Amtrak and Greyhound that has been converted into a Guantanamo Bay–style outdoor prison. The men are interrogated, strip-searched, and thrown into a cage in the parking lot. None of the men is read his rights and none is allowed a phone call. None is even charged with a crime, other than one comment about stolen property and a few incongruous remarks about al Qaeda and the Taliban. Two of the men with Zeitoun are white, but the other is an acquaintance from Syria, Nasser Dayoob. To make matters worse, Nasser has $10,000 in a duffel bag. He distrusts American banks and so keeps his life savings hidden in cash, which he has been carrying for fear of looters.

After three days in the cage, all four men are bused to a maximum-security prison, where Zeitoun remains isolated from the outside world for another two weeks. Finally, Zeitoun is able to get the attention of a passing Christian missionary, who hesitantly takes Kathy's phone number from him. Kathy, who has begun to seriously consider the possibility that her husband died in New Orleans, immediately hires a lawyer, only to find out that there is no stable legal system in place in flood-ravaged Louisiana. When Zeitoun finally gets a bail hearing, in a small cinderblock room at the prison, he is told the charges: "possession of stolen property valued at $500" (278). Bail is set at $75,000, which his lawyer will later note is "about a hundred times what it should be" for such an insignificant crime (282).

A trial is set, but, in another Kafkaesque twist, Kathy is told by unidentified officials over the phone that the location is "private information." When she finally learns the details and shows up with a handful of character witnesses to vouch for Zeitoun, the trial is canceled without explanation. It is not until the end of his third week in the maximum-security prison that Zeitoun is finally released on bail. The other three men are held until the following year. Nasser spends six months in jail and, upon release, is told that there is no record of his $10,000.

Again, the plot drives the book forward. The story opens several days before the arrival of Hurricane Katrina, and the first section generates tension through a steady stream of news reports about the approaching storm. The primary focus, however, is on the two protagonists, as they take care of their children, help clients secure their homes against yet another hurricane, and weigh the seriousness of the incoming threat. Throughout these activities, the reader learns crucial details about their past and comes to see each person's dominant personality traits.

One of Zeitoun's most distinguishing features is what Kathy calls his "exasperating . . . sense of destiny" (199). Alternatively, she describes him in the opening pages as "inexplicably solid" (8), a phrase that captures something of the intense, at points almost absurd will that drives Zeitoun in many areas of his life. His determination is perhaps most immediately notable in his work ethic. One flashback shows Zeitoun during his earliest days as a contractor in New Orleans, riding a ten-speed bike to work. His tire pops twenty minutes before the opening bell, when he is still four miles away from the job site. Rather than call in sick or simply show up late, something he had never done before, Zeitoun puts the bike on his back and starts to run. Even one bad day, he muses, could sour a relationship with a potential boss or customer, and "the consequences could be far-reaching. Work was a pyramid, he knew, built on day after solid day" (27). He is so hardworking that Kathy, when she cannot pressure or trick him into taking a vacation, leaves with the kids by herself.

Zeitoun is equally committed to his Islamic faith, and he both freely quotes from the Qur'an and consults the text regularly. The story itself is occasionally punctuated by inset quotes from the holy book. Zeitoun also remains committed to his prayers, even under the watchful eye of prison guards who suspect he is a Middle Eastern terrorist. He often endures these hardships without complaints, and his first impulse when confronted with emotional challenges is to withdraw for reflection. After their oldest daughter was born, for instance, the new parents returned home tired and happy. As Zeitoun was helping Kathy into bed, they both realized that the baby was not in the room. Zeitoun had been so preoccupied helping Kathy up the stairs of their apartment building that he had left the baby in the car seat on the lawn. He returned the sleeping baby to his wife and ran out the door before she could say anything: "He needed a walk that day, and needed walks for many days following, to work out what he'd done and why" (10).

In these regards, Kathy's judgment of her husband seems sound. Again, she imagines him as "one of those inexplicably solid, self-sufficient, and never-needy men who got by on air and water" (8). Yet he is not so stoic and introverted as to be wholly removed from their lives. Even Kathy, who has a very close relationship with the girls, is impressed by the balance Zeitoun manages to strike between firm, disciplined parenting and playful leniency: "He was not an overly doting father, and yet he never objected to them jumping on him, grabbing him. He was firm, secure, but also just distracted enough to give them the room they needed, and just pliant enough to let himself be taken advantage of when the need arose" (10). Kathy's respect for her husband is validated in scenes that reveal Zeitoun's deep emotional connection to his family. The first day of the story ends with Zeitoun watching his wife and daughters, lying in a pile before bedtime. They are collectively telling a story about Pokémon, the topic chosen by their seven-year-old daughter, Safiya. He stands in the doorway, "just watching, taking it all in. The scene was almost too much. Too beautiful. It was enough to burst a man's heart wide open" (49).

Such an expression of emotion, which might seem incongruous given other aspects of Zeitoun's character, suggests something of the protagonist's complexity. He is not simply an industrious pragmatist, that stereotypical male whose hard work and stoic façade perhaps conceal profound depths of emotion. Zeitoun's steadiness and devotion are complemented by characteristics more commonly associated with adventurous dreamers. The text opens with one of several dreams that detail Zeitoun's childhood exploits and underscore the boy's sense of wonder. The story begins by describing his first experience with the lampara fishing method used in Jableh. On moonless nights, fisherman would hold lanterns above the surface of the water to attract plankton. Then the sardines would come for the plankton, slowly gathering until there was a "solid mass of silver spinning" just below the surface of the water (3). In the dream, the thirteen-year-old Zeitoun, who has been eagerly asking questions about the work for years, goes on his first trip and is mesmerized by the "beauty of the undulating silver orb" (4).

This dream resonates on many levels throughout the book, but, most immediately, it encapsulates what might seem to be opposed aspects of Zeitoun's character. He loves the sea and spends ten years of his life traveling around the world on cargo and passenger ships. His faith does not permit him to drink or gamble, popular pastimes for other sailors, and instead he emphasizes the freedom of travel and the wondrous sights along the way (with a few brief references to women he met while traveling). The strenuous life is, of course, no problem for the hardworking Syrian. After his shifts, he often continues to work, helping out anyone who wants an extra hand. When there is nothing to do, he creates physical challenges for himself, such as swimming for three hours at a stretch in the ship's pool (145). Even the thirteen-year-old boy in the opening dream works for nothing, bringing his wages home to help the family. The whole scene concludes with a terse admission: "Abdulrahman and Ahmad didn't care much about the money. . . . They would have done it for free" (4).

The opening dream also helps to establish the context for Zeitoun's character. Not only did he grow up near the ocean, but his entire family had a "passion for the sea" (12). Zeitoun's father, Mahmoud, worked on cargo boats for years. He left the job after being thrown into the sea during a storm. After spending two days floating on the remnants of a barrel, he forbade his children to work on the sea and promised to move his family off tiny Arwad Island on the Syrian coast. After searching all over the mainland for a new house, he found an ideal two-story home. Unsurprisingly, it was less than fifty feet from the shore.

Zeitoun also has a recurring series of flashbacks about his brother, Mohammed, who was, for a brief period, the fastest long-distance ocean swimmer in the world. Mohammed began competing at age eighteen, and within two years he was winning the most prestigious international competitions. In a famous race between Capri and Naples, he beat the record time by fifteen minutes. His illustrious career was cut short by a tragic car accident. Mohammed died at the age of twenty-four, when Zeitoun was only six. In retrospect, Zeitoun knows his brother mostly through "stories, photos, and tributes, and the monument to him that stood on the waterfront in Jableh" (92). His brother's accomplishments, at least from Zeitoun's perspective, cast a long shadow over the family. He personally lives by the credo "be as good as Mohammed was" and attributes his family's accomplishments to the shared but unspoken desire to live up to his brother's legacy (116). "The Zeitouns were," he insists, "a high-achieving clan, full of doctors and school principals and generals and business owners" (12). When their father, Mahmoud, died of heart disease a few years after Mohammed's death, many in Jableh, the narrator informs us, thought that the cause was "simple heartache." The loss of his "golden son" was just too much to bear (116).

All of this history helps to explain Zeitoun's character and the various impulses that shape his vision of the world. Again, Kathy succinctly sums up his often-competing desires for achievement, adventure, and stability, his love of the wondrous spectacle and his pragmatic appreciation of that spectacle's mundane mechanics: "[Zeitoun's eyes] were dream-filled, but discerning, too, assessing—the eyes of an entrepreneur. He could see a run-down building and have not only the vision to see what it might become, but also the practical knowledge of what it would cost and how long it would take" (11). This dual vision also helps to explain why Zeitoun stays in New Orleans after the flood. He certainly feels a strong desire to watch over his home and nearby properties. Dozens of friends and clients have also left keys with him, a reflection of the great trust and respect that many afford him (54). It is also clear that Zeitoun is fascinated by the effect of the storm on the city around him. During his first canoe trips through the flooded city, he vacillates between the perspective of an adventurer who appreciates "the novelty of the new world" and a builder who clinically assesses the extent of the damage around him (96).

Zeitoun's religious background also leads him to see the destruction in biblical terms, and he comes to feel that his own presence in the city is not accidental. God, he tries to explain repeatedly to his worried wife, has a plan. All of these factors, coupled with his own drive for achievement, come together when he encounters a reporter with a camera boating around the city. After a brief interview, Zeitoun paddles away, hoping "that his siblings might see him like this, on the water, a sailor again, being useful, serving God" (167).

As should be apparent from these examples, most of Zeitoun's activities are detailed in a limited third-person point of view. The reader experiences events along with the protagonist and has access to some of his thoughts and reflections. Interspersed with these sections are others, written from the same point of view, that focus on Kathy. While Zeitoun is off helping clients make preparations for the storm, Kathy is busy managing both household tasks (preparing lunches, driving the kids to school) and much of the office work for their business. She serves as Zeitoun A. Painting Contractor LLC's "secretary, bookkeeper, credit department, [and] public-relations manager" (6). On the story's opening day, accounts of the storm grow increasingly threatening, and Kathy is forced to decide whether to uproot the children for several days while the storm passes. As she wrestles with the prospect of joining her sisters in Baton Rouge, fragmented memories from her troubled childhood take a more prominent role in the text.

Kathy grew up in a working-class neighborhood, one of nine children in a 1,400-square-foot house with one bathroom. Though few concrete details are provided, her life was so unpleasant that she ran away from home for the first time at about age six, an act that she repeated a dozen more times. School offered little solace, as Kathy attended an overwhelmingly large middle school where she was "picked on, pushed around, gawked at," in part for being "one of a handful" of white students (59). Being unhappy and quick tempered only exacerbated her problems. She left home as soon as she could and moved in with her childhood friend Yuko. They both got jobs at the same Dunkin' Donuts. By the time she meets Zeitoun, when she is twenty-one, she is divorced and working two jobs, with a one-year-old at home.

The overwhelming chaos and instability in her life drive her toward a major change. Kathy is raised as a Southern Baptist and, even as a single parent working fifty hours a week, finds time to attend a nearby evangelical church.

When Yuko, who is also a devout Christian, begins to read books about Islam, Kathy is shocked. After Yuko converts, however, Kathy is struck by her friend's newfound composure. Yuko has managed to find a sense of calm and balance that her life has long lacked. Kathy's gradual conversion underscores several of the main messages that develop throughout the book as a whole. First, Kathy's quick reaction to Yuko's interest in Islam and Islamophobia more generally at other crucial points in the text are depicted as the product of ignorance and intolerance. In a brief summary of her early readings, Kathy underscores the similarities between Islam and Christianity. Both, for instance, are "filled with the same people . . . Moses, Mary, Abraham, Pharaoh, even Jesus," and Muslims view the Qur'an as a fourth Holy Book, one that follows the Old Testament, the Psalms, and the New Testament (61).

Second, Eggers depicts Islam as a religion of openness and tolerance. Kathy is "knocked . . . flat" to learn that the Qur'an repeatedly reaches out to "other, related faiths" (61), and the conversion process itself is merely reciting a simple pledge of conviction. In contrast, the preacher at her own church scoffs when Kathy brings up the subject of Islam: "he made a snorting, derisive sound, the sort of sound an eight-year-old boy would make on a playground. . . . Did he not know that his God and Islam's were one and the same. . . . Allah is just the Arabic word for God. Even Christians speaking Arabic refer to God as Allah . . . this man, preaching to a thousand impressionable and trusting parishioners, didn't know, or didn't care, that Islam, Judaism, and Christianity were not-so-distantly related branches of the same monotheistic, Abrahamic faith. And to dismiss all of Islam with a playground sound? Kathy could not be part of what that man was preaching" (66).

This dismissiveness also recalls other common themes in Eggers's works, including the need to respect the uniqueness of individual circumstances and the importance of bearing witness, a phrase Zeitoun uses in the text. The book as a whole serves to record the Zeitouns' difficult experiences, and it is littered with important moments of acknowledgment. Zeitoun serves as a witness in flooded New Orleans, noting the storm's destruction and the challenges that many people face in the aftermath of the flood. When Zeitoun has been trapped in prison for weeks without any way of notifying the outside world, a missionary's willingness to stop, however briefly, and acknowledge Zeitoun radically changes his situation. His family receives confirmation of his whereabouts for the first time, and his release is greatly accelerated. For Kathy, the evangelical preachers represent those closed-minded people who refuse to listen to others or even consider the different lives they lead. Shortly before converting, she recalls a preacher interrupting the service to shame people for their meager donations that day. After the twenty-minute lecture,

Kathy is "aghast" at both the crassness of the appeal and the clear disconnect between the clergy and the congregation: "The congregants were not wealthy people, she knew. This was a working-class church, a middle-class church. They gave what they could" (63).

As in Eggers's other texts, this emphasis on individuality and tolerance extends beyond various identity categories (religion, race, ethnicity, sexuality) to a more generalized appreciation of uncertainty. In *Zeitoun*, Kathy praises her imams' willingness to acknowledge their own limitations and the value they placed on other's opinions. When she asks a question they cannot answer, they acknowledge it and often turn to the Qur'an with her to search for answers. Her Christian teachers, in contrast, "spent a good amount of time talking about who would and wouldn't go to hell, how hot it burned and for how long" (66).

If the text does demonize a particular kind of Christian teaching, it is always careful to stress the connections between Islam and other major religions, thus avoiding the appearance of wholesale proselytizing. Kathy also stresses the diversity of Islam, a move that further distances the religion from any one ideal representation (and, not coincidentally, responds to totalizing post-9/11 representations of Islam as a terrorist sect). In a lengthy discussion of how she had misunderstood the religion as monolithic and fanatical, Kathy notes, "There were passive Muslims, uncertain Muslims, borderline agnostic Muslims, devout Muslims, and Muslims who twisted the words of the Qur'an to suit their temporary desires and agendas. It was all very familiar, intrinsic to any faith" (62). Among these options, Yuko opens Kathy's eyes to a lifestyle that is, given her troubled past, very appealing. She is drawn to "the sense of dignity and purity embodied by the Muslim women she knew. To Kathy they seemed so wholesome, so honorable . . . they were disciplined. She wanted that sense of control. She wanted the peace that came with that sense of control" (67).

Kathy, unsurprisingly, expresses similar sentiments when she describes Zeitoun's initial appeal: "Zeitoun turned out to be everything she had not believed possible: an honest man, honest to the core, hardworking, reliable, faithful, devoted to family. And best of all, he very much wanted Kathy to be who and how she wanted to be, nothing more or less" (17). Both Islam and Zeitoun provide her, though certainly in different ways, with a sense of stability and affirm her dignity as an individual. She admits, for instance, to being "weight obsessed" as a young woman, until Zeitoun encouraged her to deal with her issues and "eat like a normal person" (40). Throughout the text, she praises Zeitoun for his support and affirmation. In contrast, members of her family repeatedly question her decisions and minimize the choices she makes. Even though Kathy converted to Islam before meeting her husband, her mother repeatedly suggests that her conversion was an act of submission, an imposition on her "true" self. When Kathy shows up with the kids in Baton Rouge, her mother immediately mentions her hijab: "Why don't you take off that thing and relax. . . . He's not here. Be yourself" (106).

After just four days in Baton Rouge, Kathy is so distraught that she sneaks out with her kids at 6 A.M. and begins driving to Yuko's house in Phoenix, nearly 1,500 miles away. In contrast to Kathy's difficult and judgmental family, Yuko arranges for Kathy to stay with a friend in Houston, while her husband, Ahmaad, flies to Texas. Ahmaad takes over the driving and travels all night, stopping only once, so they can reach Phoenix the next day. These kinds of bonds are often described in familial terms throughout the text, though they clearly do not depend on an actual biological connection, and their importance cannot be overstated. Kathy and Zeitoun are depicted as sharing a similar bond. On an average day, they call each other repeatedly to talk "about everything—painting, the rental properties, things to fix and do and pick up, often just to say hello" (16). Similarly, members of Zeitoun's family, though they live in different countries all around the world, talk regularly. When Zeitoun disappears in New Orleans, different relations, even those who do not speak English particularly well, call Kathy to get the latest news.

Beyond expanding the text's perspective on religious, gender, and family issues, Kathy's narrative serves another important function. It allows Eggers to comment on increasingly hyperbolic news accounts after the floods. Throughout the second section of the book, as Kathy is traveling from New Orleans to Baton Rouge to Houston to Phoenix, the often racially charged news stories grow increasingly alarmist. Three days after the storm hits, Kathy turns on the news and comments, in a voice that could belong to either Kathy or the narrator, "the media consensus was that New Orleans had descended into a 'third-world' state. Sometimes this comparison was made with regard to the conditions, where hospitals were not open or working, where clean water and other basic services weren't available. In other instances, the words were spoken over images of African American residents wilting in the heat . . . or standing on rooftops waving for help" (109). Accounts of deprivation are accompanied by stories of unchecked violence and crime throughout the city. The following week, the mayor and the New Orleans police chief go on Oprah Winfrey's television show to talk about people who had sought shelter inside the Superdome. The mayor says that people "got to this almost animalistic state, because they didn't have the resources. They were trapped." The two men then go on to talk about "babies getting raped" and "hooligans" killing people (175).

These media accounts serve as a perverse variation of the protagonists' desire to bear witness and help others. Kathy repeatedly expresses reluctance to believe the "hyperbolic and racially charged news coverage" (109), and many of the accounts she hears, even those that come through the chief of police and the mayor, prove to be false. Zeitoun also expresses misgivings about the news, pointing out, for instance, that "since the attacks in New York . . . every time a crime was committed by a Muslim, that person's faith was mentioned, regardless of its relevance. When a crime is committed by a Christian, do they mention his religion?" (37). Eggers does not try to deny the difficulties that many faced in New Orleans. Zeitoun does on one occasion see a group of armed men looting a gas station, and, when Kathy tells him about the news stories, he does note that things could be worse in other parts of town. This book is, after all, an attempt to reconstruct only what Zeitoun saw and did while in New Orleans. The media, however, come off repeatedly as sensationalist and misguided in the book.

In contrast to Kathy's removed perspective, Zeitoun is completely cut off from the media and provides a startlingly close perspective on a city under water. He often attempts to capture the otherworldliness of his surroundings through mythic or biblical references, emphasizing the vast difference between pre- and post-flood New Orleans. A wholly submerged motorcycle appears as a "relic from a previous civilization" (97), and a group of unattended horses seems downright "hallucinatory" to Zeitoun (155). He has to grow accustomed to "the new physics of this world," a place dominated by water and weather (97).

After he spends a few relatively tranquil days paddling around the city, ominous signs gradually begin to appear. The water grows increasingly polluted. Zeitoun sees a dead body for the first time. When he finds the bodies of a dozen or so dogs, all shot in the head, he begins to worry: "perhaps something had changed irrevocably. That this was considered a sane or even humane option signaled that all reason had left this place" (157). The second section of the book ends two days later. Zeitoun is at his own house, talking on the phone with his brother, when a half-dozen armed people in bulletproof vests burst into the building.

The brief third section of the book comes entirely from Kathy's view after she has lost contact with Zeitoun. Over the next two weeks, she wrestles with hope and fear, trying to keep the children and Zeitoun's family from sensing her panic. Just when she finally begins to consider the possibility of continuing her life without Zeitoun, a missionary calls and tells her that her husband is being held at a maximum-security prison in St. Gabriel, Louisiana.

The fourth section of the book returns to the scene of Zeitoun's capture and a vision of a new world, one dominated by a military system gone horribly wrong. In the closing section of the book, Eggers points out that the Federal Emergency Management Agency (FEMA), which was responsible for the government's response after the hurricane, had actually been "folded into" the Department of Homeland Security after 9/11. What is more, all soldiers and law-enforcement agencies working in New Orleans received a brief speculating on "terrorist exploitation of a high category hurricane" (308). Kathy understandably worries about what it means to be a Muslim and for Zeitoun to be a Syrian-born Muslim in post-9/11 America. The text underscores her worries with repeated stories about Kathy or Zeitoun being singled out. She even "half-jokingly" warns Zeitoun that soldiers are "trained to kill people like you." Her ultimate fear is that her family will "become collateral damage in a war that had no discernible fronts, no real shape, and no rules" (252).

The force of Eggers's criticism in the book is not aimed at the United States as a nation, the government as such, or even the particular individuals involved in Zeitoun's imprisonment, though all share some responsibility for the events that unfold. Instead, he targets the broken system, a system that was quickly fashioned under pressure from hysterical media coverage, the real needs of people trapped in an underwater city, and a vast military apparatus with virtually unchecked powers. The broken system, Eggers implicitly argues, coerces individual complicity and dehumanizes all involved. One of the book's epigraphs, a quotation from Mark Twain, succinctly encapsulates this aspect of the narrative: "To a man with a hammer, everything looks like a nail" (xiv).

When Zeitoun and his friends are taken to a newly constructed makeshift prison in the parking lot of a local docking station for Amtrak and Greyhound, a place that comes to be called Camp Greyhound, he marvels at the speed with which such a prison had to be constructed. It was fully operational just a week after the flood. Zeitoun speculates that it would have taken four or five days to build the cages, even with an ample supply of workers. After a major flood, finding a fraction of that labor would have been a major challenge. In addition, it would have taken time to plan the structure, gather the materials, and have supplies sent to high ground in a flooded city. Zeitoun concludes, "It was a vast amount of planning and execution. A regular contractor would have wanted weeks to complete this task, and would have used heavy machinery. . . . It was mind-boggling. It was all the more remarkable given that while the construction was taking place, on September 2, 3, and 4, thousands of residents were being plucked from rooftops, were being discovered alive and dead in attics" (226–27). Later in the text, the narrator provides a darker gloss on the building of Camp Greyhound: "The portable toilets were available and working at Camp Greyhound while there were no working bathrooms at the Convention Center and Superdome a few blocks away. Hundreds of cases of water and MREs were readily available for the guards and prisoners, while those stranded nearby were fighting for food and water" (311).

In another grim comment on the perspective informing the supposed disaster relief, Kathy conservatively speculates that at least 28,000 guns are being brought to New Orleans by law enforcement, private security firms, and soldiers (195–96). The sheer number of people and weapons leads Kathy to wonder about the origins of the trouble in New Orleans. She asks, "Was it the residents or was it those sent to bring order?" (194).

These details contextualize Zeitoun's experiences in the weeks after he is picked up. He and four other men are taken back to Camp Greyhound, where they are questioned and strip-searched before being thrown into a cage in the parking lot. Inside the station, Zeitoun counts "about eighty personnel and at least a dozen assault rifles within a thirty-foot radius" (211). The only other people there at the time are two other prisoners in a cage. Again, neither Zeitoun nor his companions are formally charged with a crime, read their rights, or allowed a phone call. While Zeitoun will ultimately be charged with "possession of stolen property valued at $500" (278), the police make no attempt to look for stolen property when they arrest him, and, Eggers subsequently learns, they never returned to the supposed crime scene. Zeitoun's own experiences are supplemented by other stories scattered throughout the text, such as that of Marlene Maten. Maten, a seventy-three-year-old diabetic deaconess, was staying at a hotel with her eighty-year-old husband. She went down to retrieve food from their car and was arrested on suspicion of possessing stolen property. She too was forced to sleep on the concrete parking lot at Camp Greyhound and spent two weeks in a maximum-security prison before charges were finally dropped (259).

The book counters these scenes of harsh and dehumanizing treatment with many moments of individual bravery and compassion. Early in his wandering, Zeitoun finds a seventy-year-old woman who weighs more than two hundred pounds clinging to a bookshelf in her home. She has probably been trapped in the water for twenty-four hours or more. When Zeitoun cannot get her into the canoe by himself, he has to go looking for help. At a main thoroughfare, Zeitoun screams and waves as more than ten boats carrying police and soldiers go past without even acknowledging him. In a more subtle symbolic comment, their wake nearly tips his canoe. It is not until two young men pass in a small fishing boat that Zeitoun gets assistance. They agree to help him immediately, and, when they finally drive off with the woman, Zeitoun realizes that they never even exchanged names. In one final comment that resonates throughout the book, Zeitoun shudders at the woman's suffering and notes that "the situation had stolen her dignity, and it pained him to bear witness" (103).

Such moments of (anonymous) compassion and generosity appear throughout the text, and they repeatedly underscore the importance of individual dignity. In contrast, the military helicopters knock over Zeitoun's tent, and the noise of the fanboats that the soldiers ride obscure the cries of those people they are ostensibly there to help. Even when they do try to help, they often display little sensitivity to the circumstances of citizens. As a helicopter draws near to offer Zeitoun water, he tries to wave the soldiers off. They ignore his signals and rain water bottles down on him from the air. Zeitoun has to leap out of the way as the falling bottles knock his tent down. Rather than record Zeitoun's emotions, Eggers concludes the scene with striking understatement: "Satisfied, the helicopter tilted away and was gone" (127).

Eggers uses a variety of different metaphors and symbols to capture the abstract structural problems that are driving the inhumane treatment Zeitoun experiences. Comparisons with machinery abound, and, while he is at Camp Greyhound, the text repeatedly draws attention to the power source for the makeshift military camp. An Amtrak train engine, "operating at full power on diesel fuel," is generating electricity. Zeitoun describes it as a "monstrous grey machine, easily a hundred tons, adorned with a small red, white, and blue logo" (219–20). The engine, later described as both "moaning and ravenous" and "devouring," reflects the broken system that is impersonally consuming those it is supposed to help, serve, and protect. The whole process, importantly, has been given an official stamp of approval by the American government. Alternatively, the prisoners at the appropriately named Camp Greyhound are repeatedly referred to as animals, a reflection of the way this system dehumanizes them.

Throughout the early days of his detainment, Zeitoun continuously reiterates his amazement at the turn his life has taken: "Zeitoun was in disbelief. It had been a dizzying series of events—arrested at gunpoint in a home he owned, brought to an impromptu military base built inside a bus station, accused of terrorism, and locked in an outdoor cage. It surpassed the most surreal accounts he'd heard of third-world law enforcement" (218). After Camp

Greyhound, Zeitoun is taken to a maximum-security prison, where he is denied medical care, let out of his cell only to shower, and periodically strip-searched. It is important to note, again, that the brunt of Eggers's criticism does not fall on the individuals involved, though they are often described in strikingly negative ways, nor is it aimed at particular institutions. Eggers, for instance, points out in both the text and his own concluding comments that the prison itself is not centrally responsible for Zeitoun's treatment. First, Zeitoun was not officially under the charge of the prison. He was under the supervision of FEMA, which had rented space at the prison for its own activities. In addition, Eggers notes that it is generally "a very well-run prison, a progressive and rational place. . . . I don't intend to denounce the operation of that prison; perhaps the institution was simply overwhelmed after Katrina and fell short of its higher standards" (335–36).

Instead, Eggers is criticizing "systemic ignorance and malfunction . . . this wasn't a case of a bad apple or two in the barrel. The barrel itself was rotten" (307). Similarly, racism remains a constant and exacerbating force in the text, but Eggers underscores that it was not the motivating factor in this case. He even tracked down the officers whose names were listed on Zeitoun's arrest report and interviewed them. Without dismissing race altogether, he is willing to conclude that "these two police officers had not purposely hunted and arrested a man because he was Middle Eastern" (307). Accordingly, Zeitoun hopes not for a radical change in the government or military at the end of the text. He simply wants a return to a more sensible form of order.

While a systemic adjustment is certainly needed in the days after Katrina, Eggers, in typical fashion, is quick to point out that sensible routines can do as much to cause problems as to solve them in unusual or unexpected circumstances. Throughout the first part of the book, Zeitoun is driven to ignore the storm by his past experiences and the pressures of the moment. As reports of the storm grow increasingly dire, he dismissively comments, "There seemed to be a half-dozen named storms every August, and they were rarely worth the trouble. This one, named Katrina, would be no different" (7). The text might ultimately highlight a system's shortcomings, but the individuals who constitute that system are never free of individual responsibility. As Eggers points out in an interview with the *Colorado Review,* this kind of injustice is "not even banal, really, so much as it is routine, and driven by a lack of courage and imagination more than anything else."[6] Again, tolerance, understanding, and compassion are required to counterbalance such shortcomings.

Given this complex message, it is fitting that the text does not end with the happy return of Zeitoun, a closing that would imply that the grave injustices have been rectified. Instead, the short final section jumps forward three years to show Zeitoun and Kathy still struggling to get past the traumatic events of 2005. Kathy is haunted by memory lapses and disorientation that doctors diagnose as posttraumatic stress disorder. Zeitoun has changed his behavior patterns to avoid places that might bring back traumatic memories. Early in the text, Kathy says that Zeitoun could live on air and water, but he loses a lot of weight in prison and, symbolically, struggles to regain it afterward. Similarly, Zeitoun continues to reassess responsibility for the events after Katrina, and he comes to accept more of the blame for his terrible predicament. He was, after all, the one who had "refused to leave the city. . . . But then something else had overtaken him, some sense of destiny. Some sense that God had put him there to do His work, to glorify Him with good deeds. It seemed ridiculous now" (262). In the closing pages of the text, Eggers reiterates Zeitoun's view: "He was ashamed. Ashamed that his hubris, if that was what it was, had caused all this" (296). It is important to note that, on this point, the text again promotes an attitude of humility and uncertainty. It underscores Zeitoun's attitude while also qualifying it with the clause "if that was what it was." Again, Eggers nods to Zeitoun's willingness to acknowledge his own limitations, even as he resists laying down a textual judgment that would seem to convey the true will of God.

After suggesting the lingering damage that the events of the book have caused and filling in some historical details, the text ends with Zeitoun ruminating on rebuilding his own life, his marriage, and the city of New Orleans. Lee Siegel, in his review of *What Is the What,* points out that both *What* and *A Heartbreaking Work of Staggering Genius* end with "the same Yes! to life, the same thankfulness for every simple day, the same feeling of blessedness and gratitude, the same vow of wakefulness and strength."[7] This description could easily be applied to the end of *Zeitoun,* as well. At the close of the book, Zeitoun declares, "There is much work to do, and we all know what needs to be done. We can only do the work. . . . So let us get up early and stay late, and, brick by brick and block by block, let us get that work done. If he can picture it, it can be. This has been the pattern of his life: ludicrous dreams followed by hours and days and years of work and then a reality surpassing his wildest hopes and expectations. And so why should this be any different?" (325).

Siegel's criticism of *What* recalls the difficult issues with which this chapter began (the relationship between fiction and reality, politics and art, and an author and his or her subject matter). Though the parameters of the debate have changed, as have the tenor of the arguments, these same topics have continued to inform conversations about Eggers's texts. This continuity is partially a function of critical discourse, but it also reflects some continuities in Eggers's work. While the focus and scope of his books have changed radically over the past decade, he does regularly return to particular issues, just as he has created a number of male protagonists who have, in a few notable ways, similar perspectives on the world.

CHAPTER 6

Short Stories, Short Short Stories, and Films

Story Collections

Eggers published his first collection of short stories, *How We Are Hungry,* in 2004.[1] The book consists of fifteen stories ranging from a title followed by five blank pages to a sixty-page story about a woman climbing Mount Kilimanjaro, which many critics have read as a nod to or a rethinking of Hemingway's celebrated story "The Snows of Kilimanjaro." This diverse and ambitious collection has been well received, and a few of the individual pieces have been widely praised by critics. The lengthy mountain-climbing piece, "Up the Mountain Coming Down Slowly," is often cited as the most successful work in the collection and has received near-universal acclaim.

One easy way to frame these pieces is by placing them in the context of Eggers's career. This collection makes sense, both artistically and thematically, as a product of the years between the publication of *You Shall Know Our Velocity* and that of *What Is the What.* The opening stories in particular often seem like extensions of Eggers's previous novel. They focus on American protagonists, placed in a global context, who are wrestling with anxieties and fears that they cannot fully articulate. The opening story, "Another," could be a reworking of the Egyptian trip that Will and Hand never get to take. A man, vaguely characterized as in late middle age, is having a midlife crisis of sorts and has agreed, for no apparent reason, to deliver a package in Egypt. The volatile political climate and the danger it poses to American tourists do not seem to be the only reason he has taken the job, but they do make it more appealing. After dropping the package off at the airport, the man employs a guide to ride with him, on large black Arabian horses, to a pyramid. The trip becomes an occasion to meditate on mortality and human connectedness, as two strangers hurtle through the desert toward a tomb that has long since been stripped of its treasures.

The second piece, a two-page short short story, centers on a similarly positioned man who has been suffering from "untouchable ennui" (17). His already fragile world is further shaken when he begins to ponder, as the title puts it, "What It Means When a Crowd in a Faraway Nation Takes a Soldier Representing Your Own Nation, Shoots Him, Drags Him from His Vehicle and then Mutilates Him in the Dust." He seems surprised to discover that this incident feels "personal" (18), when so many other deaths, happening much closer to his home, seem to affect him far less.

The third story, "The Only Meaning of the Oil-Wet Water," literally returns to the world of *You Shall Know Our Velocity.* Pilar, a dermatologist who runs into Will and Hand briefly at a hospital in the novel, travels to Costa Rica to meet Hand, who has "traveled widely in the past few years, since a trip with a mutual friend of theirs, now dead, had brought him halfway around the world in a week" (29). Pilar, the narrator states, "was fleeing nothing" and is quite clear about her intentions: "At thirty-one she was still unmarried and Hand was one of her few old friends also still unmarried, and the only attractive old friend she'd never slept with" (23). The story begins with an air of inevitability. Pilar has gone on such trips before and insists that the lead-up to sex is the same every time, a claim largely borne out by the action of the story. "The simple and only question" for her is "would they want to continue having sex?" (24).

The story tracks Pilar's thoughts as the relationship progresses, drawing attention at key moments to her "forced metaphors" and broad generalizations. In a parallel way, the narrative is littered with ominous moments that are unrealized and apparent symbols that may be irrelevant. When the couple runs across a group of horses outside their hotel, the narrator asserts, "the horses had no symbolic value" (32). (Eggers used a similar statement, which calls attention to the potential symbolic value of the horses even as it denies that very value, at the end of Hand's interjection in *Sacrament.*) The author Joanna Briscoe, in a review of *Hungry,* views both strands as a reflection of Eggers's desire "to demonstrate that life can be mundane, disappointing and bewildering, and our search for symbolism and significance may be only that."[2] The story's meditations on gender, relationships, travel, and desire ultimately move toward Pilar's concluding reflections on God and a statement that has appeared, though with slightly different inflections, in both *You Shall Know Our Velocity* and *Hologram:* "The oil-wet water was not God. It was not the least bit spiritual . . . it felt perfect when Pilar put her hand into it, and it kissed her palm again and again, would never stop kissing her palm and why wasn't that enough?" (52).

If the first stories in *Hungry* involve characters who are confronted by the unfamiliar in various ways, the unfamiliar in each story, much like in *You Shall Know Our Velocity,* remains secondary to the protagonists' development (or lack of it). The longest story in the collection, "Up the Mountain Coming Down Slowly," begins similarly, as a story about a woman named Rita who has arranged to climb Mount Kilimanjaro. Rita feels that she has spent "so many years . . . doing everything in her power to finish but again and again and again she has pulled up short, and has been content for having tried. She found comfort in the nuances between success and failure, between a goal finished, accomplished, and a goal adjusted" (191).

The story, however, shifts as Rita slowly becomes aware of the porters who help hikers up the mountain. At first she is impressed by a hiker who can speak bits of their language, something that she has clearly never considered doing. Then, she has a startling realization that these men are simply at work, with families waiting in towns below. The hikers also begin to notice the porters' difficult working conditions. Many of the men wear the same clothes day after day, regardless of the weather, and Rita sees a group of men huddled around a tub, waiting for the communal bowl of porridge that will presumably constitute their entire dinner. At the end of the story, Rita learns that a group of porters has frozen to death sleeping in a tent with a giant hole in the side. Struggling with her own complicity in their deaths, she bounds down the mountain alone. The story ends with Rita in the ranger's station, adding her name to the long list of those who have climbed Mount Kilimanjaro. (The story is followed by a rather sententious piece, "When They Learned to Yelp," that deals with young Americans supposedly belated awareness of true pain and misery.)

Another way to frame this collection is through its title or, more specifically, the often-inexpressible desires and anxieties that haunt the stories' protagonists. Each of the stories described is motivated in part by the characters' confused and conflicted needs. "Climbing to the Window, Pretending to Dance" covers similar ground, with a nod back to *A Heartbreaking Work of Staggering Genius.* The story, which could be read as a more focused variation of Eggers's relationship with his suicidal friend John in the memoir, features a protagonist named Fish. Fish is torn between his desire to help a cousin who has just attempted suicide for the seventh time and his anger at being forced to play a role in the demeaning drama. After discovering that his cousin jumped off a roof that was only about eighteen feet high, Fish moans,

"There are too many things wrong everywhere for this kind of shit" (75). Yet the narrator also longs for "the community of souls" and laments losing faith in the idea after being duped out of $20 by a well-dressed man at a gas station.

Such notions of connection and community echo throughout the volume and continue Eggers's meditations on engagement from *A Heartbreaking Work of Staggering Genius* (the "lattice") and *You Shall Know Our Velocity.* "Notes for a Story of a Man Who Will Not Die Alone" is about a man who wants to make his death beautiful by turning it into a social event, attended by hundreds or even thousands of people. The story, as the title suggests, is written in the form of an author's notes, which generate tension as the piece slowly moves toward the staging of the final death scene.

Eggers's willingness to foreground formal inventiveness, a trait far more characteristic of his early writing than of more recent work, also unites many of these pieces.[3] The most widely lampooned piece in the collection, "There Are Some Things He Should Keep to Himself," consists of five pages that are blank except for page numbers and the title in the header. (The piece was excluded from the paperback edition.) "Your Mother and I" is a tongue-in-cheek account of how a couple spearhead numerous initiatives that have "improved" the world, from creating a "badass" UN peacekeeping force that ends genocide to eliminating billboards and painting Kansas purple. The piece is narrated by a man preparing a meal with his daughter and formally unites the preparation of the meal, the "creation" of a better world, and procreation. (Much to his daughter's dismay, the narrator repeatedly alludes to sexual activity with his wife.) The final story in the collection, "After I Was Thrown in the River and Before I Drowned," is told from the perspective of a dog, who recounts, with much joie de vivre, the days leading up to his death.

The other long story in the collection, "Quiet," revolves around a rendezvous between two friends. Tom has flown from Washington, D.C., to Scotland to spend the a few days on the Isle of Skye with Erin. As in "Oil-Wet Water," the meeting starts as an innocent flirtation. The two travel through the rainy countryside while Tom muses about Erin's beauty and secretly hopes that they will be stuck in a hotel room with only one bed. The narrative takes a turn when Erin accidentally reveals that she once had group sex with two of their coworkers, men who had made a pact with Tom not to pursue her. In a fit of rage, Tom leaves Erin at a hotel and takes a rowboat out on the water.

The narrative takes another turn when the boat springs a leak and Tom is forced to swim more than five hundred yards to shore. Intoxicated with his own masculinity, Tom drives back to get Erin and begins drinking whiskey, which he'd "always loathed but now felt was the only appropriate drink for someone like [him]self, someone who could save his own life" (108). From this hypermasculine perspective, Erin seems like a rat, someone who "would mate with whomever or whatever she shared a cage [with,]" and Tom wants to "stroke her like a pet" (108). The narrative builds toward a brutal sexual encounter that casts both Tom's idealized chivalry and his manly posturing in a new light. The conclusion stands in sharp contrast to that in "Oil-Wet Water" and, like "Up the Mountain," provides another indirect consideration of Hemingway's fictional and historical legacy.

Amid these longer stories are five short short stories, each of which is less than two pages in length. They all focus on the psychology of individual characters, and four of the five involve heightened states of emotion. Each documents a small revelation or admission that Eggers, in an interview about a later collection of short shorts, claims "wouldn't or couldn't find its way into a novel, and which didn't warrant a longer story."[4] Along with "A Soldier Representing Your Own Nation," the pieces involve a man who is reconsidering the direction of his life after meeting a new woman, a mother who realizes that she is looking forward to yelling at her son and a woman considering the future implications of sleeping with a man that she has brought home from a party. The other piece, "On Wanting to Have Three Walls Up Before She Gets Home," is driven by a man's earnest desire to impress his wife. As the title suggests, he makes the admittedly arbitrary decision to erect three walls of a small house for their child in the hope of pleasing her.

Over the next few years, Eggers published two more collections of microfiction. *Short Short Stories,* released by Penguin in 2005, collects a number of pieces Eggers did for the London *Guardian. How the Water Feels to the Fishes* came out in 2007 as part of a boxed set, *One Hundred and Forty-Five Stories in a Small Box*. The collection also includes Sarah Manguso's *Hard to Admit and Harder to Escape* and Deb Olin Unferth's *Minor Robberies.* Eggers's two collections contain twenty-four and thirty-one short pieces, respectively, and have only two in common ("On Making Someone a Good Man By Calling Him a Good Man" and "What the Water Feels Like to the Fishes"/"How the Water Feels to the Fishes").

The pieces contained in these collections are not radically different from the short fiction included in *How We Are Hungry.* Many focus on individuals and depend on slight twists or revelations to generate narrative movement. "The Horror," from *How the Water Feels to the Fishes,* is about a woman named Sandra who avoids horror stories because "the line between fiction and reality, for her, was much too malleable."[5] When she turns thirty, however, she becomes interested in developing a horror story, one that, it turns out, defies the conventions of the genre. As Sandra thinks through her plot, she decides that it will take place during the day and that nobody will die. It will have only the pretense of suspense, and characters will wander around talking laconically, "eyeing each other and every doorway warily." In the final lines of the three-page story, the "horror" plot has become nothing more than a reflection of mundane existence, with characters who "walked calmly through their lives, without threats, without suspense or shadows, expecting nothing and revealing nothing" (22). Such a scenario would itself be, Sandra concludes, horrific.

In their simplest form, such twists serve as little more than punch lines, as in the two-sentence opening piece, "Once a Year": "Once a year, she remembers that she is insignificant. Then she forgets again, because more than she is insignificant, she is forgetful" (5). Such pieces often aim to elucidate odd moments for or the curious traits of unusual characters. Occasionally, Eggers moves away from progressions, twists, and reversals to spin out a quirky thought over several pages. "Old Enough" features an unnamed narrator listing things he would do if he were, in fact, old enough. The three-page list, which often veers toward the absurd, includes his desire to "draw conclusions and burn bridges," "tell untrue stories of his time in Algeria," "burn himself alive," and "study whales, become better with the whales than almost anyone" (8–10). After spinning out this thought process without apparent direction, the piece gives itself some semblance of structure at the end by joining the last discussion of whales with an earlier discussion about complimenting physiques. The narrator hopes to meet "young researchers with their young bodies and tell them all about the whales and their bodies, how magnificent they all are" (10).

The title piece, "How the Water Feels to the Fishes," combines several of these elements, while also moving away from the more typical focus on individual characters, to create a touching meditation out of a seemingly absurd premise. The story begins with fish, which are "always happy to oblige," attempting to explain how water feels. The imaginative setup (a collective human "we" interrogating seemingly wise and introspective fish), the surprising question (how does water feel to a fish?), and the creative replies ("like powder touching ash"; like "the cleanest tooth") all combine to create a striking opening that draws on a theme common in Eggers's work: the difficulty of articulating the fundamental or elemental aspects of existence. After several responses, the fish surprise the narrator by asking about human curiosity. Why, they wonder, would anyone want to know what water feels like to fish? When the narrator cannot explain, the fish change tactics and ask about the feeling of air. Again, the narrator falters, and the piece ends with the fish gently guiding people toward more thoughtful responses. Both the curious questions and the odd metaphorical comparisons invite further interrogation. Moreover, the surprising relationship between fish and humans gives the piece a touch of pathos that is sometimes lacking in stories that must be developed over a handful of sentences. It is, finally, a story that employs devices used in many of the other pieces but to somewhat different effect. (The earlier version, published in *Short Short Stories,* has a different final sentence, one that draws attention to the fundamental difference between the fish and the narrator rather than the developing relationship between fish and humans).

Eggers's microfiction fits with his other short stories from this period and can be alternately or simultaneously humorous and dramatic, realistic and absurd. In the final story of *How the Water Feels,* "Steve Again," he even draws on a character from the last story of *How We Are Hungry*—the dog Steve. At the end of *Hungry,* Steven drowns and begins running through the afterlife, a clean but apparently empty landscape watched over by God (the sun). In "Steve Again," a dog named Steve is running along a cliffside "which may or may not be the end of the world" (60). Steve realizes that he has seen enough and turns back to find the right audience for his story.

Films: *Away We Go*

Eggers collaborated with his wife, Vendela Vida, on the script for *Away We Go,* his first major creative role in a film project. The movie, directed by Sam Mendes (*American Beauty*), was released in the summer of 2009 and stars John Krasinski (*The Office*) and Maya Rudolph (*Saturday Night Live*). Shot for an estimated $17 million, far less than the $100 million budget his next project would receive,[6] this modest film follows two thirty-somethings, Burt and Verona, as they prepare to have their first child. The pregnancy, which was unplanned but not entirely unwanted, has forced the couple to take a long look at their lives and to reassess their place in the world.

Burt and Verona have been together, it appears, for quite some time, and they are deeply committed to each other, though Verona has repeatedly refused Burt's proposals. "I just don't see the point," she declares at several different moments during the film. Burt also reveals that she has expressed misgivings about having a ceremony without her parents. Her mother and father died while she was away at college. It is unclear whether or not this is a legitimate concern or a strategic dodge (don't disrespect my dead parents!), but Verona has struggled with their deaths and seems shaken by the realization that they will never get to meet their granddaughter.

Burt's parents live near the couple. Jerry and Gloria, however, are not particularly invested in the birth. At the beginning of the film, they announce that they will be leaving for a two-year stay in Antwerp just one month before the baby is born. Burt and Verona, who moved to the area to be close to his parents, are shocked. As a consolation, Gloria offers to let the young couple use their house, if, that is, they are unable to rent it out before they leave. (The agent calls Gloria before the end of dinner to let her know that he has found a tenant.)

This news sets the story in motion, as Verona quickly realizes that there is no longer anything tying Burt and her to their current residence. The couple does not have very much money, which is made clear through shots of their cluttered, underheated little home with a cardboard-covered window. At the same time, both of their jobs could be done from anywhere. Burt, who never graduated from college, sells insurance over the phone, and Verona is a medical illustrator. It does not take long for the couple to agree, and they quickly draw up a plan to visit friends and relatives in Phoenix, Madison, and Montreal.

The episodic narrative brings Burt and Verona in contact with a wide range of families and parenting styles, an experience that forces them to reconsider their fears and hopes for the years ahead. Burt is a dreamy optimist, who is excited about the baby and fantasizes about a "Huck Finn-y" childhood. He wants their daughter to "run along streams and know how to work a canoe. Be able to entertain herself outside." The more practical Verona has little enthusiasm for such visions and worries instead that they are "fuck-ups" who lack direction. These very different personalities complement each other well throughout the film. Verona is often overwhelmed by their situation, but Burt is always there to offer kind and humorous words of support. Similarly, he is prone to drifting off on visionary tangents, and she must take responsibility for the pair. She even staples their itinerary to the inside of his coat.

As the two travel, it becomes apparent that other models of family life will be of little assistance to them. The first two couples they encounter, after Burt's flighty and self-absorbed parents, are appalling caricatures. In Phoenix, Lily and Lowell take the couple to a dog track. Lily drinks constantly, blathers embarrassingly about her life, and ridicules her children. She openly mocks her son's large ears ("Did you see them? He looks like a trophy") and is convinced that her twelve-year-old daughter is a lesbian because of her "tough girl" walk. Lowell, who has just learned that the couple did not get accepted into the "good" golf club, broods throughout the day and caps off dinner with a monologue about the coming droughts that will bring about the end of humanity.

In Madison, they meet one of Burt's childhood friends, Ellen. Ellen, a professor with a large trust fund, has rechristened herself LN and spends much of the encounter expounding on her personal philosophies. She and her husband, Roderick, joined the "continuum movement," which aims to counteract the alienation and despair children experience in the world with familial closeness. The family shares everything, including one large bed, and avoids the "three s's," separation, sugar, and strollers. The clearly satirical encounter includes a passionate speech about male pregnancies in the "seahorse community," LN's declaration that childbirth has allowed her to understand war, and a number of incongruous references to literary and philosophical works.

In Montreal, the tenor of the film changes when the couple meets Tom and Munch, who seem to lead an ideal life with their four adopted children. The family's playfulness is apparent from the moment Burt and Verona try the doorbell. The old buzzer has been modified so that the ring is followed by a scream, as if the bell were electrocuting someone inside the house. In the family room, the children dance and sing along with the "end" of *The Sound of Music*. It turns out that Tom and Munch have excised the Nazis from the film to help "the kids live a few more happy years." Dinner provides yet another striking contrast to the previous encounters. The children eat pizza and frolic about the house while their father praises their creativity. The two couples then go out to a jazz club, and Munch stresses the importance of balance: "the kids want you there but not all the time. They need air as much as you do."

Before they even reach the club, Burt and Verona declare Montreal the winner and raise a cheer for the city that could be their new home. Their happiness, however, is quickly disrupted by two unforeseen tragedies. As the evening progresses, Tom and Munch grow increasingly emotional until Tom reveals that his wife just had her fifth miscarriage. It turns out that the only thing missing from their happy family is a biological child. Tom laments the selfishness of people who wait until their thirties to start having kids and bemoans the unfairness of a world where "a million 14 year olds get pregnant without even trying." His moving speech ends with a declaration that echoes through the remainder of the film: "It is terrible feeling this helpless."

Before Burt and Verona have even had a chance to process this information, the couple gets called to Miami, where Burt's sister-in-law has just walked out on his brother and their young daughter. Both of these situations remind the couple of life's unpredictability, the different and often difficult circumstances that face every couple, and their own love for each other. Though Verona insists again that she will never marry Burt, they end their evening in Miami agreeing to impromptu vows about parenting and their future relationship. These events also presumably cause the couple to rethink their approach to finding a new home; the final scene of the film finds them driving alone to Verona's parents' place on the water. The large house, which Verona and her sister had been renting out, will now be their home.

This final decision marks both Verona's acceptance of her past and the couple's willingness to step out on their own and create a new life together. As they drive up, she says that she wants the road both to look familiar and also to be new, "new for us, new enough to feel like we found it." While the ending does mark a development, particularly for a woman who has long been worried about being uncool and a "fuck-up," the movement is tenuous. The couple are just beginning their new life, and, in the final shot, they sit alone on the porch as the sun comes up. The unpredictable events of the day are still ahead. In the film's final moments, Burt turns to Verona, optimistic as ever, and says, "This place is perfect for us. Don't you think?" As if to underscore the uncertainty of the future, Verona avoids pat assurances and closes the film with an expression of desire: "I hope so. I really fucking hope so."

Critical responses to *Away We Go* have been split. Many reviewers struggled with the contrast between the film's affectionate treatment of its protagonists and its broad satirical swipes at other couples. A. O. Scott's review in the *New York Times* challenges the story's "smug self-regard" and concludes with the memorable warning "this film does not like you."[7] Similarly, Richard Corliss's review at Time.com bears the title "*Away We Go:* We're OK, You're All Idiots." Others praised the film's attempt to be more than a story about the difficult transition to parenthood or yet another picture about couples attempting to find a home in the world. In its unusual melding of road trip, unplanned pregnancy, and midlife coming-of-age story, the film attempts, as the reviewer Stephanie Zacharek put it, "to map a certain kind of contemporary listlessness: Burt and Verona are people who are grown up enough to have babies, but they don't have particularly fulfilling jobs or live in a place they really like. They don't feel connected to the world around them in any meaningful way, and they're just not sure what to do about it."[8] It is a film that ultimately tries to find hope for a couple without overlooking the very serious difficulties that they face in the world. If the vision might feel a bit too insular to some, it is also ambitious in its focus on a particular kind of contemporary experience, one that remains underrepresented in major motion pictures.

Where the Wild Things Are

In the brief acknowledgments section of his novel, *The Wild Things,* Eggers notes that Spike Jonze approached him "out of the blue one day" in 2003. Jonze wanted to collaborate on a screen adaptation of Maurice Sendak's classic children's story *Where the Wild Things Are.*[9] Eggers also implies that Sendak himself, in the middle of the scriptwriting process, first suggested the idea of creating a novel out of "all this accumulated material" (287). The book and the film both appeared in October 2009.

Sendak's original story, which is only ten sentences long, is about a boy named Max who misbehaves and is sent to bed without supper. In his room, a boat appears, and Max sails to a faraway land where he meets the wild things, large creatures with huge teeth and claws. After Max fearlessly silences the creatures and refuses to look away, they name him the "king of all wild things" and commence a "wild rumpus." The festivities conclude when Max sends the creatures to bed without dinner. Despite the fun of the rumpus, Max longs to be with someone "who loves him best of all," and he sets sail for home, where a hot dinner is still waiting for him.

The film is faithful to Sendak's original drawings and expands the narrative to feature length. Max is no longer simply a boy in a wolf suit making mischief. He is living with his divorced mother, a compassionate woman who is struggling with a demanding job, two children, and a boyfriend. Max's sister also seems to have little time for him. In a telling early scene, Max has spent the afternoon alone digging a tunnel that will serve as his fort. When his sister's friends stop by to pick her up, he pelts them with snowballs and retreats to the safety of his snow cave. The boys chase him, and one jumps on the mound, collapsing the tunnel and burying Max under a pile of snow. Max's sister barely registers the incident and the group drives off, leaving Max crying outside. In a fit of rage, he runs up to her room and begins destroying things.

To make matters worse, the next day at school his science teacher explains that the sun will one day "die," extinguishing all life in the solar system. Feeling small and helpless, Max finally snaps that evening when his mother, who is busy entertaining her boyfriend, ignores him. Seeking a way to both retaliate and express his larger frustrations, Max puts on his wolf suit, climbs on the kitchen counter, and yells, "Feed me woman!" The ensuing squabble ends with Max racing out the front door.

Sendak's text implies that Max's voyage is a psychological projection, a suggestion that the film develops further. Each of the wild things has a distinct personality, and many of these personalities are dominated by childish traits displayed by Max and other characters in the opening scenes of the film. Alexander, a small goatlike creature, is often irritated because he gets ignored by the larger beasts. Carol seems depressive and often lashes out by destroying things. In his first scene, he is upset because K.W., a motherly female beast who is unsure whether or not she belongs with the group, has left. Carol's anger clearly echoes Max's feelings of abandonment (by his father, his mother, and his sister), and he responds by destroying the wild things' houses.

Max is put in charge of these juvenile and often competing creatures and feels responsible for their happiness. As a nominal parent, Max revisits moments from earlier in the film and can reconsider these incidents from a new perspective. The wild things have a dirt clod war that echoes Max's snowball fight. The group also builds a large fort, one that Carol marks for destruction late in the movie. After Max's successive failures to bring them lasting happiness, the wild things grow surly, and Douglas, the logical bird-creature, is forced to reveal what he has long believed: "[Max] is just a boy pretending to be a wolf pretending to be a king." When Carol asks Max about his past position as a Viking king, a story Max told initially to impress the wild things, he is forced to admit, "I'm not a Viking or a king or, or anything. . . . I'm Max." This stripping down of identity marks a psychological step forward for the boy and suggests that he may finally be ready for reintegration into a larger family unit. He first tells K.W. of his intention to return home shortly after she helps him escape from a rampaging Carol. At the same moment, he demonstrates a newfound appreciation for his mother's efforts and tells K.W., "I wish you guys had a mom."

As in the original story, the film ends after Max's voyage home, but in this version his mother is waiting up for him. They embrace, and the mom, in a symbolic gesture, pulls back his wolf hood. Max eats his dinner while his mom slowly drifts off to sleep at the table, and the last shot shows Max studying her. A small smile, reflecting both his appreciation and his newfound understanding, flickers across his face.

Eggers's novel, entitled *The Wild Things,* roughly follows the plot of the movie. At nearly three hundred pages, the book does take the time to develop characters and relationships a bit more, and it often makes motivations more explicit than the film does. Max, for instance, still struggles with his parents' separation and clearly dislikes Gary, his mother's boyfriend, who appears only momentarily in the film. Several days a week, though never often enough to raise suspicion, he hides necessities in unusual places and sits back bemusedly as Gary fumbles around the house. Moreover, when he first runs away, Max plans to find his father "in the city" and move in with him. Later in the story, he reflects on his relationship with his father, who "phoned on Wednesdays and Sundays but sometimes did not" (7). There is only a pull-out bed at his father's apartment, and his dad has a boring girlfriend named Pamela. As Max gradually matures, he realizes that his dad's place is not a realistic option for him.

Max's relationship with the wild things is also increasingly involved, and parallels are made more explicit. The story started, as Eggers mentions in the acknowledgments, "with the question of not *where* but *who* the Wild Things are, and what they want from life and from Max" (286). This shift in focus accounts, at least in part, for the shortened title of the book, and it also explains the effort to both individuate and thematically organize the wild things. In the book, for instance, it is Alexander, the small and often ignored goat-beast, that accuses Max of pretending to be king. Max initially responds by punching him into submission but quickly comes to see "at last that they were more alike than different. Their size, their fur—they were versions of the same undersized and overtrying creature" (265–66). This version adds a more explicit thematic dynamic that is only implied in the film. Not only is Max more overtly struggling with a facet of his own nature, but Alexander foregrounds the issue of identity in their exchange. After Max denies "pretending to be the king," Alexander rolls his eyes and says, "you don't even know who you are!" (262). It is this overt charge that pushes Max over the edge and leads to the beating.

Eggers's novel also foregrounds a number of other themes that remain implicit in the film. The book leans heavily on the contrast between order and chaos, often figuring Max as a chaotic force in a larger system. Max even describes his own behavioral problems in terms of cognitive dissonance: "Every so often Max felt his thoughts could be straightened out. . . . But there were other times, other days, most days really, when the thoughts did not line up. . . . And it seemed that when this happened, when he couldn't make sense of something, when the thoughts did not flow from one to the other, that on the heels of the scattering quail he did things and said things that he wished he had not said or done" (33–34).

Eggers is also very intent on capturing the uncertainties of adolescence in the text, and he carefully plots Max's development over the course of the story. Early on, Max is driven by anger and frustration, and he has a difficult time articulating a positive direction for his life. His father has given him a "want journal" for just such a purpose. Some time after the fort incident, Max picks up the book and fashions grim tortures for Gary, his sister, and all of her friends. He quickly remembers, however, that his father had forbidden him to include "negative wants." After some reflection, he rearticulates his hopes: "I WANT to get out of here. I WANT to go to the moon or some other planet. I WANT to find some unicorn DNA and then grow a bunch of them and teach them to stick their horns through [my sister]'s friends" (71). These reflections help establish Max's psychological condition and provide a rationale for his subsequent journey. They also point to the existential angst that permeates Max's middle-class childhood. As soon as he sets down the journal, Max wonders, "What did he want to do? This was the central question of this day and most days" (71). It is also the "central question" that dominates his time with the wild things, as the creatures constantly look to him for a plan that will "make everything better for everyone always for all time" (156).

By the end of the story, Max is not necessarily better at controlling himself, but he does have a better understanding of the consequences of his behavior and a greater appreciation for the efforts of those around him, particularly his mother. After returning home, he knows that he is "different. . . . In some ways he felt too big for this house. But he also felt newly able to fit within it" (284). In this version, Max removes his own wolf hood and finds his mother asleep on the couch. The setup almost seems to deliberately recall a young Dave Eggers hovering over his dying mother in *A Heartbreaking Work of Staggering Genius*. Here, recast by imagination, the young boy stares tenderly at his mother, who is peacefully asleep. Max removes her glasses and gently brushes the hair from her face. The story concludes with a reflection on Max's developing perspective: "He stood above his mother for some time, knowing her now, really almost knowing her now, happy to watch her rest" (285). This statement captures Max's desire to understand and feel closer to his mother, even as it qualifies his knowledge, pointing to the inevitable gap between individuals that haunts much of Eggers's work. All of Eggers's major texts could be described, in some form, as character studies, and many explicitly probe the formal and epistemological conditions that govern their own creation. *The Wild Things* is certainly a more personal novel than many of Eggers's recent works, but it does not depart wholly from his recent concern with the relationship between the individual and larger social and institutional orders. It also fits well with Eggers's tendency to explore the impact of personal tragedy and, more particularly, individuals' efforts to make meaning out of loss.

CHAPTER 7

A Hologram for the King

A Hologram for the King revolves around Alan Clay, a divorced fifty-four-year-old salesman now working for Reliant, "the largest IT supplier in the world."[1] He and three other Reliant employees half his age have traveled to Saudi Arabia in order to demonstrate the company's new hologram technology for King Abdullah. An employee in London will be able to "appear" at the meeting, move about the room, and converse with those in attendance. No other company in the world has such advanced capabilities, and the hope is that this demonstration will convince the king to award Reliant contracts, potentially worth hundreds of millions of dollars, to provide services for a new city being built on the Red Sea. King Abdullah's Economic City or KAEC, as it is often abbreviated, is intended to be a majestic port and economic center that would help "diversify the Middle East's largest economy" (47). King Abdullah, known as a reformer, has suggested that the city will provide many opportunities for Saudi men and new freedoms for women.

Alan, who knows nothing about the technology they are selling, has been brought along in part because he had met the king's nephew twenty years earlier. The company hopes that the connection will be of some use in negotiations. Alan also used to be known as a man "who could get things done." He fondly remembers working at Schwinn, where he climbed the ladder from "retail sales in downstate Illinois to the regional sales office, to a place at the table with the execs in Chicago, planning strategy and expansion" (80–81). He also recalls some of the perks of his privileged position, including a seemingly guaranteed income and weekend fishing trips to Lake Geneva with the VPs.

Those days, however, have long since passed. Schwinn, in part under Alan's strategic guidance, moved its operations to China. When asked about the company's decisions by a young businessman, Alan succinctly summarizes the situation: "How did your suppliers become your competitors? That was a rhetorical question. You want your unit cost down, you manufacture in Asia, but pretty soon the suppliers don't need you, do they? Teach a man to fish. Now the Chinese know how to fish, and ninety-nine percent of all bicycles are being made there, in one province" (49).

After the Schwinn brand was sold off, his opportunities slowly disappeared. At the moment, Alan acknowledges, he "was as intriguing to corporate America as an airplane built from mud" (11). Before contracting with Reliant, he was making about $22,000 a year running a one-person consulting firm out of his house, a house that he is desperately trying to sell to pay for his daughter's tuition at "a very good and expensive college" (4). Between the obligations, a volatile relationship with his ex-wife, Ruby, and a strange growth on the back of his neck, Alan feels defeated. At home, one of his favorite pastimes is watching the Boston Red Sox's World Series victories in 2004 and 2007, particularly the game in which they hit four consecutive home runs against the New York Yankees. He has "watched those four and a half minutes a hundred times and each viewing brought him something like joy. A sense of rightness, of order. It was a victory that could never be taken away" (11).

The trip to Saudi Arabia offers Alan a similar opportunity. The commission from the contract would pay off his debts, provide for his retirement, and allow him to take care of his daughter. It would be, in short, a major victory that would bring order to his life again. Yet, at the opening of the novel, he struggles to escape the malaise that has gripped him. On his first day in Saudi Arabia, he wakes up late and misses the shuttle to KAEC. When he calls the team, he cannot even "muster the energy" to lie about his absence (7).

Alan's absence turns out to be of little concern. The king is not even in Saudi Arabia, and no one seems to know exactly when he is planning to visit KAEC. His schedule is kept secret from almost everyone, even many of his own employees, for security reasons. The Reliant representatives have little choice but to prepare every day, in an outdoor tent with faulty air conditioning, for a meeting that could happen at any time with little advance notice. The epigraph for the book ("It is not every day that we are needed") comes, appropriately, from Samuel Beckett's *Waiting for Godot,* a play about two men waiting for a mysterious figure named Godot who never arrives. Similarly, *Hologram* records Alan's activities as the days slowly pass. In a gradually evolving internal monologue, he wrestles with past choices, ponders ways to save his crumbling family, and reconsiders a globalizing world that seems to have little need for him. In addition to Beckett's play, critics have compared the work to both Kafka's oblique allegories, which feature characters trapped in systems that operate beyond their understanding or control, and Arthur Miller's *Death of a Salesman,* a play about the decline and eventual suicide of salesman Willy Loman. These references should suggest something of the tenor of Eggers's novel, a brooding story in which the most significant plot point, the arrival of King Abdullah, occurs in the last chapter and is wrapped up in less than four pages.

A Hologram for the King can also be usefully compared to other texts in Eggers's oeuvre. It illustrates certain elements that have remained constant throughout his career and others that have developed significantly over the past decade. Most of Eggers's major texts, for instance, involve protagonists who are dealing with trauma. Many of his books have also been preoccupied with Americans reconsidering their role in the world. In *A Heartbreaking Work of Staggering Genius,* the "world" is defined in relatively narrow terms and the perspective is chiefly personal (as opposed to, say, political, economic, or historical). In subsequent work, Eggers began to focus more directly on the interaction of individual voices and larger social structures. *You Shall Know Our Velocity,* in some ways the most direct antecedent to *Hologram,* places white midwestern twenty-something men in a series of global settings that challenge their perspectives. *What Is the What* and *Zeitoun,* though they continue to focus on the ways in which individuals process catastrophic events, move beyond the perspective of the white American man and draw attention more directly to the political and economic systems that constrain individual action. *Hologram* builds on these later explorations by foregrounding concerns about globalization, even as it implicitly recasts Eggers's early work with particular kinds of self-conscious white male protagonists.

Yet the author is not simply concerned with how people struggle inside larger social systems. He is also interested in how these interactions are captured, shaped, and/or transformed through language and narrative. *A Heartbreaking Work of Staggering Genius* could be described as the story of an author-figure meditating on the process of writing about a narrator who is reflecting on past events. The prose style is accordingly varied, as the story follows the author through moments of self-doubt about the process of writing to manic bursts of emotion that accompany troubling memories. Through Eggers's subsequent books, his conceptual experimentation and his preoccupation with the role of the author in the text have become less overt, going from the fictional world constructed around *You Shall Know Our Velocity* to the self-justifying paratexts of *What Is the What* and *Zeitoun. Hologram* extends this pattern by engaging with a fictional character very unlike the actual Eggers and treating thc issue of creation primarily at the thematic level.

The novel also continues a trend in Eggers's recent works toward increasingly sparse prose. *Zeitoun* utilizes a reportorial style, transcribing the events and thoughts of its protagonists with little overt editorializing or contextualization (at least until the later pages of the book). This style, as Eggers has suggested, draws the audience's attention to the characters and events, not the author or his writing process. *Hologram* also employs a stripped-down writing style and a focused form of narration, but, interestingly, it does so to almost opposite effect. The sparseness of the writing leaves much to the imagination of the reader and draws attention both to the gaps in the text, those things which are not or cannot be directly stated, and to the story's larger implications.

The writing, which many have compared with Hemingway's pared-down style, is terse and direct, at times even surprisingly so. When Alan first mentions his daughter, for instance, he encapsulates the situation and a long stretch of his own personal history in a few sweeping judgments: "[Alan] did not have the money to pay her tuition for the fall. He could not pay her tuition because he had made a series of foolish decisions in his life. He had not planned well. He had not had courage when he needed it. His decisions had been short sighted. The decisions of his peers had been short sighted. These decisions had been foolish and expedient" (4). Alan's opening declarations create narrative intrigue by referring obliquely to events that will be dealt with in greater detail later in the text, a strategy common in Eggers's books. Yet this passage stands out precisely because of the way in which it is written. These statements, both blunt and sweeping, do not simply introduce specific moments in the novel's plot. They draw the readers' attention to questions of motivation and responsibility, and they point toward a larger historical perspective, one that includes the potentially sweeping category of Alan's "peers."

This passage is also immediately preceded by another generic reference: Kit's unnamed but "very good and expensive college." When the unusual style is coupled with such abstractions, the novel takes on a generic and almost allegorical air. The last name Clay, which recalls accounts of God making man from a lump of clay, potentially positions Alan as an "everyman," a figure who could represent a certain kind of "average" American for readers. Eggers underscores this possibility when Alan first sees his own reflection in a balcony door. Writers often use chance reflections to describe a character's appearance while remaining within that character's point of view. Eggers, however, does not describe any of Alan's (potentially individuating) features.

Instead, the reader simply learns that "[Alan] looked like an average man. When shaved and dressed, he passed for legitimate" (12).

The epigraph pushes readers in a similar direction. *Godot* itself is an oblique allegory that has led generations of viewers to speculate about the mysterious title figure. The particular passage Eggers has chosen comes from a speech that invites a broader symbolic reading of Beckett's play: "It is not every day that we are needed. Not indeed that we personally are needed. Others would meet the case equally well, if not better. . . . But at this place, at this moment of time, all mankind is us, whether we like it or not."[2] The reader of *Hologram* is ultimately being pushed to consider more than the historically specific moments depicted in the text. Eggers seems to suggest, without moving the narrative entirely into a symbolic register, that characters and institutions and events may have larger historical resonances.

More specifically, Alan's personal history is bound up with the accelerated pace of globalization in the second half of the twentieth century. Alan moved with Schwinn when it moved manufacturing operations from Chicago to (nonunionized) Mississippi, and he even took the lead when it tried to convert a Soviet-era factory in Budapest to a "Schwinn-owned, capitalist model of efficiency" (45). Then the industry shifted its attention to Southeast Asia, Taiwan, and China. Within a few short decades, the Chinese, Alan notes, have already begun moving some manufacturing to Africa. One of Alan's former acquaintances sums up the situation with a pointed quip: "manufacturing should be on a perpetual barge, circling the globe for the cheapest conditions possible" (13).

Alan feels torn about these developments. His father, Ron, a union man who retired with a full pension before his company headed south to lower labor costs, is quick to point out that Alan "had contributed *not insignificantly* . . . to all that undid Schwinn and the 1,200 workers employed there" (82). To a certain extent, Alan seems to agree with these charges. One of his primary sources of debt comes from an attempt, after the effective demise of Schwinn, to "pioneer a new line of bikes—classic, durable, for the collectors and the tinkerers and the families who just wanted something indestructible" (135). The new line was to be manufactured in Massachusetts. Alan suggests that the plan could be his "shot at redemption" and expects his father to be impressed. Ron merely scoffs, "You helped all that move to China. You can't put that genie back in the bottle" (136). In a grim commentary on changing conditions, Alan, who has already developed a viable business plan and commissioned a prototype, is laughed out of every bank he approaches about a loan.

At the same time, Alan resists accepting full responsibility for Schwinn's collapse. These business decisions, he suggests, were driven by economic forces that even large companies could not resist. To an imaginary interlocutor, Alan fumes, "Do you know how hard it was to hold out even that long? To try to make bicycles, very complicated and labor-intensive machines, on the West Side of Chicago, in a hundred-year-old factory, until 1983?" (51). Alan, who is now being displaced by the very system that he, in some ways, helped to create, struggles to assess both his role in the process and the evolving world order. Ron, who has retreated from the modern world to a small farm in New Hampshire, has no patience for such ambivalence: "They're making actual *things* over there, and we're making websites and holograms. Every day our people are making their websites and holograms while sitting in chairs made in China, working on computers made in China, driving over bridges made in China. Does this sound sustainable to you, Alan?" (84).

Beyond these reflections on the global labor market, *Hologram* also draws attention to local issues in Saudi Arabia, where it seems the working class is largely composed of immigrants. Alan's driver and guide, Yousef, quips, "We don't have unions here. We have Filipinos" (41). Alan also repeatedly notes the lack of Saudis among the hotel staff, construction workers, and lower-level managers that he encounters. This economically stratified diversity is accompanied by striking divisions in material conditions. When Alan visits a largely empty condominium complex in KAEC, one of three buildings in the "city," he accidentally goes to the wrong floor. Instead of lush carpets, panoramic windows, and bright chandeliers, all of which can be found on the floor above, Alan walks into a space that reminds him of "pictures he'd seen of prison gyms converted to dormitories. There were fifty bunks, clothes hanging on lines between them." All the workers are gathered in the middle of the room, watching two people fight over an old cell phone with a cracked screen. It had been discarded by one of Alan's coworkers on their first day in KAEC (207–8).

This scene is a striking reflection of contemporary economic, political, and cultural realities. An American man, who is a temporary employee of a multinational corporation that hopes to help erect an economic center in Saudi Arabia, attempts to mediate a dispute over an outdated and, from a Western perspective, disposable object between foreign workers of unclear origins and unknown interests. Much like the protagonists of *You Shall Know Our Velocity,* Alan repeatedly draws attention to such instances of cultural confluence and disjuncture, particularly when they involve Western artifacts. On their first drive out to KAEC, for instance, Yousef, dressed in a thobe and hand-made sandals, struggles to connect his iPod to the stereo system in his "puddle-brown" Chevy Caprice.

Moreover, Alan, like Will and Hand, tends to characterize these moments as a form of temporal displacement. To Alan, Yousef's "ancient" car "sound[s] like the past" (24). Similarly, when he flees the workers' conflict and runs up to the furnished floor of the apartment building, Alan feels like "he had leapt forward in time" (210). This example reveals the unconscious values that Alan brings from his upper-middle-class life in America. The differences that he catalogs here are not strictly chronological. A chandelier is no more contemporary than a worker in a red jumpsuit. His unconscious association, however, of convenience and luxury with "the present" tends to demean those implicitly "uncivilized" things linked with the past (210). These workers and their living conditions are, for Alan, metaphorically comparable to whooping cough or polio, things that society should have progressed beyond in the twenty-first century (125).

Eggers's text does not endorse Alan's perspective so much as it tries to capture his mental process. Alan is struggling to come to terms with an increasingly complex world, and his sense of displacement in this new culture allows him to consider the implications of globalization in a new context. By foregrounding Alan's observations and the startling discoveries he makes in Saudi Arabia, *Hologram* draws attention to the systems that underwrite "progress" and the seemingly disposable people who help those systems run. Alan, after all, would never have seen the living quarters of those workers had he not gotten "lost," a word that he ponders uncertainly after emerging into the luxurious "present" of a finished apartment. In addition, he might not have been able to consider such people at all had he himself not been thrust into such a tenuous position by global economic developments.

This play of visibility and invisibility becomes central to Alan's perspective on Saudi culture as he struggles to come to terms with a society that is both infused with modernity and resistant to developments that have already begun to take place. Alan is amazed to learn, for instance, that Yousef is exchanging texts with a married woman even though the punishment for adultery is death. Yousef explains that "all the married women" have two phones, one for their husbands to monitor and another for private business. Alan concludes, "the whole country seemed to operate on two levels, the official and the actual" (119). Later a European woman tells Alan that she received an official warning from the coast guard because she went swimming in a bikini. In the liberal city of Jeddah, however, she did not get into any real trouble: "they look the other way in most cases, but they want to know where you're doing whatever you're doing. Mostly so they can be assured that other people don't *see* you doing whatever you're doing" (175).

Eggers presses this contrast between appearance and reality even further in his reflections on contemporary manufacturing. There used to be, as one of the king's functionaries puts it, "real international competition, where you were choosing between very different products with very different heritages, sensibilities, manufacturing techniques." A French bike, for instance, was different from an American one because they were produced by different people in distinct places, each made with its own materials and techniques. Now, however, "it's a matter of putting different stickers on the same bikes. They're all built in the same handful of factories" (49–50). In a globalizing world, true cultural difference is being replaced by features that have been deliberately designed and constructed for audiences in different places. The situation in Saudi Arabia reveals the disparities that still exist between cultures, but Alan's emotional reflections on local production suggest just how much the U.S. economy has shifted in a few short decades. Local production, common less than a half century before, has now become part of a sentimentalized past.

Given this tension between appearance and reality, the hologram, a figure that is both present and absent, becomes a powerful symbol that resonates through various levels of the text. Alan, who can be seen as a hologram-like figure, struggles throughout much of the novel to engage with the world around him. He also worries that others, especially the "young people" from Reliant, see him as superfluous. His worry seems at least partially justified. Alan spends much of his time at KAEC wandering the grounds or sitting with his feet in the ocean. On a larger level, Alan's career seems to be in a comparable state. He maintains the illusion of working, with an official consulting business and a handful of contacts who occasionally suggest opportunities, but he does little actual work, and his role in Reliant's latest endeavor is tenuous at best. Eric Ingvall, the Reliant VP in New York, has serious doubts about Alan's competence. At an early meeting, he bluntly asserts, "I need reassurance that you're the right man to send on this. . . . You've been on the sidelines for a while, and I need to know you're sharp. That you're a gamer" (64). Alan's primary asset is his former relationship with the king's nephew, and even he is doubtful that this distant connection will be of any help in Saudi Arabia (11).

The book's conclusion, a brief chapter that details the king's arrival, keeps these issues in the foreground. After having spent weeks waiting in a tent outside the main office building, the Reliant team is prepared and executes a flawless demonstration of cutting-edge hologram technology. The king and his entourage clap politely and leave without speaking to anyone, presumably to meet with representatives from a Chinese company *inside* the main offices. (A group of vans with Chinese writing on the side, which Alan has never seen at KAEC before, show up just in time for a meeting with the king.) Three days after the presentation, Reliant's contact at KAEC, Karim al-Ahmad, comes out to the tent to inform Alan that "the contract to provide IT to the new city had gone to another firm that . . . could deliver the IT far quicker and at less than half the cost" (311). With this stunning blow, Alan realizes that Reliant's presentation may have been little more than a business formality for the king, perhaps to create the illusion of a competitive bidding process. The city of KAEC, after all, could itself be a mirage. At the moment, it consists primarily of three buildings in the desert.

On a more literal level, the hologram serves as an extension of current developments in social media. It simulates face-to-face interaction with others but only in a way that is heavily mediated by technology itself. It is a form of contact that can seem both strikingly immediate and strangely remote. Alan relies on the potential distance offered by technology in communications with his ex-wife, Ruby. In order to "cordon . . . off the chaos" (74), Alan and Ruby exchange information only through short e-mails. (They have agreed to a maximum length of three lines.)

In short, the hologram symbolically encapsulates many of the technological, social, and economic developments that *Hologram* as a whole foregrounds in its narrative. Ironically, many of these developments are prefigured by Alan's own early work as a salesman, where his job was to create illusions, or perhaps, to put it more precisely, to transform people's perceptions of reality in order to sell products. Despite recent changes in the marketplace, which are making men like Alan obsolete, he maintains his admiration for great salespeople and repeatedly refers to art and magic when discussing them. His mentor, Joe Trivole, whom he compares to "a hypnotist or magician," shows him that "there were people in the world for whom the world and its people were subjects on which to cast spells" (72).

Joe teaches Alan much about this process of cultivating illusions for customers. In particular, he helps Alan develop an easy and superficial familiarity with strangers. On his first day as a door-to-door salesman, for instance, Joe stops Alan as he reaches for the doorbell: "A stranger rings, a friend knocks, he said. The door opened" (71). While this final terse sentence literally refers to the customer's door, it also suggests something more abstract, a door in Alan's mind. These teachings changed his perspective and helped him develop a style that would prove to be highly successful. When Alan leaves Fuller, where he worked with Joe, he freely admits that he "brought the same lessons to bike sales. All the principles applied" (80). Decades later, Alan still relies on (and can parrot) Trivole's precepts.

Again, Eggers does not blame Alan directly for global economic and industrial developments. He does, however, suggest that Alan is complicit in the system on a variety of levels. As a result, the text does not merely valorize an idealized preglobal past, as Ron might, but draws attention to the complex, interrelated processes, operating over many decades, that have brought Alan to a desert in Saudi Arabia. Like many of Eggers's other books, *Hologram* not only suggests Alan's limited role in larger social and political systems but also emphasizes the limited perspective that he or any individual can bring to current events. Alan is often at a loss to explain the actions of those people who are closest to him, such as his ex-wife and his father, much less the larger global systems that shape the contours of their lives. The narrative, which is rooted in Alan's point of view, even moves outside his perspective at particular moments to point out what he does *not* know.

After one more or less typical day at KAEC, Alan rides home with "the young people, all of whom slept on the way home, or pretended to sleep" (133). This comment reflects both Alan's feelings of isolation and his inability to distinguish between reality and imitation. Back at the hotel, the four disembark, "more or less wordlessly," and Alan is left to wander the hotel. He eats a steak alone and retreats to his balcony, where he watches "a few figures" struggling to cross a busy highway below. This tense moment could serve as a symbolic counterpoint to Alan's lonely futility, but he is either unwilling or unable to construct such an interpretation: "[The figures] made attempts, retreated. The traffic was moving too fast. Finally they made it, rushing and weaving, and Alan had learned nothing" (133).

While Alan feels like an insignificant and powerless observer through much of the text, the locus of his frustration changes. He blames himself, his wife, the tumor in his neck, and a range of abstract forces and systems. The credit rating agencies, for example, serve as the subject of one diatribe. After a mix-up leaves Alan with an unpaid $32 balance at Banana Republic, the company sends the bill to a collection agency. When Alan realizes the mistake, he immediately pays the bill, but not before his credit score sinks "50 or so points below what would qualify him as trustworthy or even human" (137). This low score, despite Alan's protestations and any evidence he can submit to demonstrate his credit-worthiness, are what finally prevent him from being able to get a loan for his bike business. Alan concludes, "The age of machines holding dominion over man had come. This was the downfall of a nation and the triumph of systems designed to thwart all human contact, human reason, personal discretion and decision making" (139).

If the "system," an abstraction that Eggers's text works to complicate, often seems to deny the possibility of meaningful action, it is important to note that the text does not retreat entirely into Kafkaesque slipperiness. Guidebooks and marketing reports certainly struggle to keep pace with the changes of modern life. In one passage that seems to come directly out of *You Shall Know Our Velocity,* Alan asserts that "conveying cultural norms was like reporting traffic conditions. By the time you published them they were irrelevant" (22). Attentive and intelligent people, however, are able to make sense out of apparent chaos. Dr. Zahra Hakem, one of Alan's love interests late in the book, perceptively suggests that the king, who has recently been selling far more oil in Southeast Asia than in the United States, might want to give the KAEC contract to a Chinese company.

Similarly, the despondency and restlessness that appear throughout the text come from characters who feel trapped or restricted and do not necessarily reflect authorial defeatism. Bright young Saudi men see little opportunity to find meaningful work in their country, and Saudi women are forced to navigate a host of regulations on social interaction. Alan, a door-to-door salesman who adapted his style to "get things done" in corporate America, worries that he may no longer be necessary in an age dominated by multinational corporations, the Internet, and holographic communications. All of these characters, however, are trying to think about how recent developments create and limit opportunities for change. Alan repeatedly asks people why the king does not simply fund the building of KAEC himself. While this question seems perfectly reasonable and people are disarmed by its simplicity, there are many complicated issues involved. Can one person, even a wealthy king, force broad cultural change or transform a national economy? Even if the king spends a fortune building the city, what will it take to get people and businesses to populate it? How will others in the region react to this supposed center of "Inter-Arab financial cooperation" (47)?

No one is able to provide an answer to Alan's question, and the open-ended narrative offers no easy solutions for these characters. Yet the story remains, finally, open ended rather than simply defeatist. Alan tries to remain optimistic. He "wanted to believe that this kind of thing, a city rising from dust, could happen" (39). This optimism, however, flags at many points in the text and often seems to be little more than a well-honed reflex for a skilled salesman. Others, such as the pragmatic driver Yousef, provide alternate perspectives. He suspects that KAEC is "already dead." The king is eighty-five, and Emaar, the global developer involved with the project, "was going broke in Dubai. Everything was overvalued and now they're busted" (38–39). Yousef, who links the global financial downturn with misperceptions and illusory values, will not accept Alan's rosy assessment of KAEC until he can see the city being built. When for the first time the two approach the three isolated buildings that make up KAEC, some workers are sweeping the road in front of them. Yousef laughs and comments, "this is where the money's going. They're sweeping the sand in a desert" (42).

As this last comment suggests, Eggers connects discussions about appearance/reality and individuals/systems with a larger debate about the relationship between people and nature. KAEC, after all, aims to be a thriving metropolis full of Venice-style waterways in the middle of a desert. At one extreme in this debate is Alan's former neighbor, Charlie. Charlie discovered Transcendentalism and, over a period of two years, left Alan letters and clippings from books that, among other things, touted the importance of connecting with nature. Then, one cold September morning, Charlie walked slowly into the lake by their homes. It took hours, but Charlie finally froze to death, an action that Alan wants to interpret as a final act of communion. Ron, Alan's father, represents a slightly less extreme version of this retreat from modern life. A smart and sophisticated man who knows "a good deal about French food, wine," Ron now eats meat and potatoes, leers at women on the street, and reeks of algae from the water in a small lake that he dug on his property (82–83). This "caveman" reversion does not seem like a viable alternative to Alan, either, even though he admits that his dad "seemed stronger than he had in decades. His face was ruddy, his eyes gloriously alive" (81).

Alan tends toward the other end of the spectrum, viewing nature as, at best, an indifferent force that will correct imbalances like "an animal that shakes off its fleas when they dig too deep, bite too hard" (102). For Alan, this challenge makes human creation even more impressive: "Looking over the valley, the work of humans so small next to the work of wind and water, Alan had the reaction he had so often, which was *people shouldn't live here*. . . . But then where should they live" (247)? In the face of tornadoes, hurricanes, earthquakes, volcanoes, and any number of other natural assaults, living strikes Alan as an "act of sheer will" against staggering odds (34).

The protagonist's resolute acceptance of hardship and his romantic vision of human struggle might be appealing to many readers, especially when compared with Ron's crass behavior or Charlie's bizarre suicide. On a more abstract level, both Ron's retreat from the modern world and Charlie's transcendent vision, his focus on a mystical "grandeur" encompassing but also beyond the material world, seem like forms of escapism. In different ways, they both evade the practical realities of American life in the early twenty-first century. This opposition, however, is not so easily resolved. Alan's focus on the practical has had, at best, mixed results. As he acknowledges in the first chapter, "his decisions had been short sighted. . . . These decisions had been foolish and expedient" (4). Moreover, Alan often finds peace precisely when he escapes from the confines of daily living. He longs to duck out of the tent at KAEC to put his feet in the ocean, feels at peace visiting Yousef's family compound in the mountains, and attains a great measure of happiness swimming in the ocean with Zahra. These moments do not necessarily swing the narrative back toward Ron's or Charlie's perspective so much as they highlight Alan's own limitations. At the close of the book, he simply stays at KAEC, waiting for an opportunity with the people who have just rejected him. This decision reflects both the difficulty of Alan's situation (what else is a fifty-four-year-old salesman to do?) and his lack of vision. Unlike, say, Yousef, who at least casually considers the possibility of revolutionary activity in Saudi Arabia, Alan never seems to consider alternative courses of action and opts, instead, to wait for a dictate from the king.

One final opposition that emerges during these considerations of nature, action, and illusion is between American and European perspectives, or at least that is how the binary is characterized by a drunken man on a plane. Those who think like Americans, in this simplified vision, are not limited by history or ancestry. They look instead to an optimistic future that can be reached through immediate action in the present. In contrast, Europeans are weighed down by history and have a presumption of decline (12–14). The drunk man, like several others in the text, worry that America has slipped to the other side and become "a nation of Doubters, worriers, overthinkers" (13). Later in the text, Alan meets an architect who has been working abroad for ten years because "in the U.S. now there's not that kind of dreaming happening. It's on hold. The dreaming's being done elsewhere for now" (143).

Alan himself wavers between these two positions, at times bemoaning the lack of possibilities and at others charging forward with reckless optimism. At several points, he even evinces a deeper desire, reminiscent of characters like Ron, to escape history. On one rare vacation, years before the action of the novel takes place, Alan relishes the time away from work, the thoughtless days "glorious for their simplicity" (163). Similarly, when Alan visits Yousef's family compound in the mountains, he is invited to go on a hunt. A wolf is terrorizing local flocks, and a group of men is going to stake out a nearby farm. On the trip, Alan insists that he sit in the back of the truck, where he will be close to nature and can mingle with locals. In short, he longs to erase national, ethnic, and class differences and to enjoy "the simplicity of being who he was: no one" (252).

At the same time, Yousef's family compound, a massive structure designed for all the villagers to use, reminds Alan that he has no lasting connection to any place in particular. He grew up in Dedham but has no connections left there. His most pressing memory of Duxbury, his current home, is that the city made him tear down a wall that he had built. The destruction of the wall is symbolic of both the power of bureaucratic systems to disrupt the creative potential of individuals and Alan's inability to construct a place for himself in the world. Alan laments this lack at several points throughout the book. At the end of the book, for instance, Zahra briefly tells Alan about her family. After she rattles off a number of places that make up her "heritage" (Saudi Arabia, Lebanon, Switzerland, and Greece among them), Alan meekly replies, "I want that, too," and asserts that he wants to "find out where everyone comes from. Every side of me. I'm going to ask around" (291).

Alan's concern with self-discovery points to another aspect of the text that is obscured a bit by the previous discussion. Mapping out the text in terms of large thematic elements positions Alan as an almost allegorical figure trapped without history in a world of high technology, consumerist illusions, and grand economic forces that operate beyond the control of individuals. While this thematic overlay does accurately capture the grim realities facing Alan, it misses the text's genuine concern with Alan as a man. By the end of the novel, the narrative is being driven in large part by Alan's personal struggles. His failure to secure a contract for Reliant seems to be a foregone conclusion in a world where everything goes to the cheapest bidder.

Accordingly, Alan's character is quite complex. He does seem, in many ways, like a decent person. He wants to do the right thing and insists on keeping his promises. He repeatedly exhorts himself to be useful, a job that he refers to as "the greatest use of a human. . . . Not to consume, not to watch, but to do something for someone else that improved their life, even for a few minutes" (180). The text does not downplay his personal faults and limitations, but it contextualizes his failings and acknowledges that he is not alone. Alan's first attempt at romantic connection in the novel involves the payroll consultant at KAEC, Hanne. On their second and last night together, the two wind up in the bathtub, where Alan stimulates her but remains unaroused himself. The chapter closes with a distant, perhaps authorial, voice that surveys the scene: "there would be a time when the world created people stronger than them. When all of this got worked out. But until then there would be women and men like Hanne and Alan, who were imperfect and had no path toward perfection" (180).

For all of his positive traits, Alan is not necessarily a likable character. His lengthy monologues and painful self-awareness could certainly make him seem whiny or self-absorbed. He is, however, decent enough, despite all of his faults and shortcomings, to leave room for debate. As a result, the novel's conclusion ultimately falls somewhere between tragedy and comeuppance, between a heartbreaking failure and a satisfying punishment for one of the shortsighted individuals who steered American manufacturing into a global morass.

Alan's personal progress is equally fraught throughout the work. In one strand of the plot, he struggles to come to terms with family conflict. Shortly before he leaves America, Alan's daughter, Kit, writes him a six-page letter condemning her mother, Ruby. Kit wants "nothing more to do with her" (73). Though the two have always fought, this declaration puts Alan in a difficult situation. His own relationship with Ruby seems nothing short of terrible. They communicate only about Kit, and even those conversations are carried out through terse e-mails. Alan has not spoken on the phone with his wife in more than two years. Yet he feels compelled to mediate this dispute and to rehabilitate, if not fully repair, Kit and Ruby's relationship. Beyond his own feelings of inadequacy and his hesitancy to become an "only parent," Alan fears that Kit might one day turn on him in a similar fashion. By "propping up" Ruby, he is, in part, protecting himself (73).

Alan also seems to have a fairly close relationship with his daughter, in part because of Ruby, whose instability has thrust Alan, who had been on the road during long stretches of Kit's early childhood, into the role of the stable parent. He is now a source of emotional and economic support for his daughter, which makes his current inability to provide for her all the more painful. Finally, Kit and Ruby's relationship represents one of the few aspects of Alan's life that he can directly influence. For all these reasons, Alan spends much of the book drafting his reply to Kit's letter. He discards each attempt, much like Will in *You Shall Know Our Velocity,* but the process helps him explore and articulate his feelings.

One other major difficulty that Alan wrestles with throughout the novel is his sense of detachment. Early in the text, Alan complains about his inability to "engage on a continual basis" (16), and he remains distant from many of the people he encounters. The opening weeks at KAEC are monotonous and isolating, and Alan's only real excitement comes when he is alone in his room. After Hanne provides him with some black-market moonshine, Alan begins going on "desperate adventures" in his own mind (171), during which he traverses the past and writes confused letters to his daughter. During a couple of these drinking binges, he takes sharp objects and probes the growth on the back of his neck, a move that could reflect Alan's sincere attempt to understand his past or suggest that the whole process is a grotesque parody of productive reflection. For Alan, it is a starting point.

His first substantial interaction with another person in the text comes after he meets Hanne. Early in the book, they attend a wild party at the Danish embassy together, the collective equivalent of Alan's drunken nights alone. Hanne pulls Alan into the garage, but he refuses to engage in sexual activity. She tries one more time, inviting Alan over for dinner several days later. He does get in the bathtub with her, but only because "he would rather extend the night with her, however bizarrely, than be alone" (174). Alan has not had sex in eight years and tries to explain to Hanne "the ease of his life without" and "the simple purity he felt, how life was altogether more streamlined now" (177). Though Hanne seems to remain interested, she stops pursuing Alan, and the two speak only intermittently at KAEC through the remainder of the text.

Alan is presented with another opportunity for development and connection when he travels to Yousef's compound. The family servant is unhappy that Alan is there, and a local man stops to ask if Alan is with the CIA. Yousef, however, is happy to have Alan, and their relationship shows signs of transforming into a real friendship, something that seems missing from Alan's life. Moreover, Alan feels rejuvenated in the mountains. When driving away from the village, he even gets out of the car to help two men build a wall, a symbolic counterpart to the wall that Alan was forced to destroy in his own yard.

While this trip initially seems like it might mark a turning point for Alan, both socially and psychologically, the mood changes quickly when Yousef and Alan agree to join the wolf hunt. Alan, who is excited to go, quickly realizes that he does not want to kill "any animal" and dreads "the moment when the wolf, hit by a bullet, would jerk, stagger about, and, immobilized, be filled with lead" (254). As they settle in above the sheep, Alan and Yousef begin talking about World War II. The war, for Alan as for Will in *You Shall Know Our Velocity,* represents a moment in time when the choice between good and evil was obvious. The battlefields of Europe provided a clear direction and opportunities for genuine heroism that seem to have long since vanished. After some reflection, Alan admits that Ron, who had fought bravely and served time as a POW in Germany, had "better stories than Alan had or would ever have" (255).

This conversation turns to the situation in Saudi Arabia, and Alan is further discouraged by his own complacency: "Alan was shaken. . . . It was the knowledge that there would be no fighting, and there would be no struggle, no stand taken, and that the two of them, because they were not lacking materially, because despite injustices in their countries they were the recipients of preposterous bounty, would likely do nothing. They were content, they had won. The fighting would be done by others, elsewhere" (259). To counteract this growing sense of impotence, Alan fixates on shooting the wolf. "To shoot a wolf in the mountains of Saudi Arabia," he thinks, "will be something. The man who pulls the trigger will have done something" (260). Long after the other men have retreated from their posts, Alan stares intently at the field, looking for any sign of movement, and he imagines the men's admiration when the deed is finally done. Before long, there is movement below, and Alan shoots at the young shepherd boy who has come to lead the sheep inside. The action reignites Alan's own sense of personal failure and a host of ethnic tensions with the men at the hunt. Yousef arranges for a driver to take Alan home the next day.

Back in Jeddah, Alan, in a more literal attempt to heal, goes to the hospital to have his tumor removed. (He still secretly hopes that his current psychological problems are being caused by the growth.) As with the wolf hunt, the surgery is interspersed with flashbacks about heroic figures and events from Alan's past. Most important, he remembers taking Kit to one of the final space shuttle launches, a scene that serves to remind readers of America's diminished present. To paraphrase the architect from the Danish embassy party, that kind of dreaming is not happening in the United States now. During the launch, a tearful Alan imagines taking up the cause: "I sold capitalism to the communists. Let me sell the Shuttle. I will help you get to Mars. Give me something to do" (276). Even full of this momentary passion, Alan knows that he has no outlet for his desires, and, in a striking anticlimax, he leaves the launch thinking about being stuck in traffic for the rest of the day. Similarly, the surgery finishes without complications, but the benign growth seems an unlikely source of Alan's problems.

In the final major episode of the novel, Alan begins exchanging e-mails with his doctor, Zahra Hakem, and the two eventually arrange to have lunch at her brother's house on the coast. Given the country's restrictions on social relations, Zahra has to arrange for a driver to pick Alan up and then send him away on errands when they finally arrive at the house. Alan, for the first time in the novel, seems genuinely excited about the prospect of a sexual encounter, and, in an odd twist, he draws strength from his own sense of insignificance: "He glanced outside, at the sun-soaked sky, at the sea unknowable, and in their vastness he found strength. A million dead in that water, billions living under that sun, that sun a hard white light among billions more like it, and thus all of this was not so important, and thus not so difficult" (298). In this mindset, Alan regrets the time that he wasted fighting with Ruby and appreciates the simple pleasures of the moment ("that smell of hot flesh—this was reward enough" [299]), a realization that is common in all of Eggers's major texts.

Despite Alan's struggles and the positive buildup, Alan and Zahra are unable to have sex. In a final comment on the limitations of the human will, the narrator notes, "they found themselves apologizing for various failures. For parts of their bodies that would not cooperate or did so only intermittently. When he was ready, she was not, and this sent him shrinking" (300). For all its attention to forms of obsolescence specific to the twenty-first century, Eggers does nod toward the more general difficulties of aging in the text. The two finally "collapse . . . tired as prizefighters" and stare out at the sea (301).

Alan and Zahra get drunk afterward while waiting for the driver to return, and Zahra says that she has to leave town for a few weeks. Alan immediately assumes that this is the end of the relationship, but the text neither confirms nor denies his suspicions. Eleven days pass between this scene and the king's arrival, but no mention is made of the doctor or of any of Alan's relationships. From the perspective of Alan's development, the continuation of this particular romance is less important than Alan's ability, at least mentally, to engage intimately with a woman. In terms of the larger narrative, the sexual failure and grim parting set up the abrupt concluding chapter.

Again, Alan's final decision to remain at KAEC and wait for a job opportunity reflects both his incredibly difficult circumstances and a distinct lack of vision. Even he worries that his prospects in Saudi Arabia are not really all that good. When Karim, his contact at KAEC, says he would like to help, Alan is surprised and thinks of the "many reasons" that Karim would not want to help him. Alan has no choice, however, but "to presume goodwill. He had to hope for amnesia" (312). The decision is finally, for Alan, an imperative, and the story closes with his determination to remain: "He wasn't being sent away, after all, and he couldn't go home yet, not empty handed like this. So he would stay. He had to. Otherwise who would be here when the King came again?" (312). This final rhetorical question presumably comes from Alan, but it moves beyond his own personal concerns to such an extent that it takes on the air of an authorial interjection. The final pages are primarily concerned with Alan's immediate prospects, but here the focus shifts to the king and his audience.

On one level, this closing recalls the text's thematic concerns with choice and action in a web of transnational bureaucracies. On another, it recalls the larger existential questions that hang over the book, those introduced with the epigraph from Beckett: "It is not every day that we are needed." Alan has chosen to wait, hoping that his future will be dictated to him by the authorities in Saudi Arabia. He needs to be needed. (This position stands in stark contrast to, say, the pose that Eggers periodically adopts in *A Heartbreaking Work of Staggering Genius,* in which he points out that a person does not find or is not given an audience. He or she must create that audience.) At the same time, the rhetorical question seems to suggest a larger imperative. Alan does not need to remain at KAEC. The king simply needs *an* audience. What would he be, after all, if nobody recognized his authority? To put this issue in the terms discussed throughout the chapter, the system works, in the final analysis, only because individuals propagate it. Industry in the United States is in its current state precisely because individuals like Alan made the choices that they did. At the same time, Alan was only ever one cog in a much larger machine, a machine that gave his life purpose and direction. But how does one go about changing the very system in which one lives? Rather than force closure on Alan's story or suggest that there is an easy way for individuals to navigate these ongoing global processes, Eggers chooses to leave the narrative open ended. In the process, he draws readers' attention to the relationship between the individual and the king, who- or whatever he may be.

This larger perspective raises several complications for the story. In the context of global economic forces, Alan's personal developments come to seem quite insignificant. If he had grown and developed a beautiful relationship with Zahra, would he be any less adrift in a transitional global economy? The jarring perspective of the final question also opens up the opportunity for readers to turn these questions on themselves. Everyone, through his or her daily actions, explicitly and implicitly supports the supposed "progress" of the current system. If recent developments seem problematic, to what extent might we be implicated in them and to what extent can we each be agents of change?

AFTERWORD

The Circle

The Circle,[1] like *A Hologram for the King*, starts with a major contemporary issue, in this case the social and psychological impact of the Internet, but develops a fictional world all its own.[2] This is to say that Eggers's most recent text seems less concerned with historical or mimetic verity than it is with exploring a particular set of ideas and their implications. Despite the work's loose parallels with major places and figures in the technology industry, Eggers has called it "pure speculative fiction" and boasted about his relative ignorance of that very industry. He has mentioned in several interviews that he never visited any "Internet campus" while working on the book, nor did he read any books about major players in the industry. He did not even speak with contemporary employees of these companies to limit the influence of actual people or events on his narrative (Guttierrez, McSweeney's).

As might be expected, critics knowledgeable about the industry have been quick to challenge the work and its various mistakes and misrepresentations. Just one week after the book was released, *New Republic* published "5 Things Dave Eggers Fundamentally Misunderstands about the Internet" (Bennett). Many subsequent reviews have repeated or further developed Laura Bennett's points from this early piece. In particular, critics have noted Eggers's misuse of the term "operating system" and his misrepresentation of technology companies' actual engagement with social media (Salmon). These criticisms, while valid, often neglect to note that Eggers's text seems less concerned with tracing actual history than it is with exploring the ways in which contemporary technology could potentially reshape the social order. For this reason, Margaret Atwood, in a largely sympathetic review for the *New York Times Review of Books,* refers to it as a "a novel of ideas" ("Privacy").

Some reviewers have challenged this very aspect of the novel, citing its flat characterization and uneven plot. Perhaps most memorably, Jessica Winter notes, "*The Circle* sometimes reads like a satire of NASCAR in which all the cars are played by freight trains" (Winter). Atwood, however, perceptively warns readers, "don't look to *The Circle* for Chekhovian nuance or thoroughly rounded characters with many-layered inwardness: it isn't 'literary fiction' of that kind. It's an entertainment, but a challenging one: it demands that the reader think its positions through in the same way that the characters must" (Atwood). This intellectual challenge is a key feature of the style itself. Like much of Eggers's recent work, the writing is relatively sparse. Most characters get little more description than a mention of hair color or a notable feature. Yet large passages are given over to arguments about characters' beliefs or justifications for particular behaviors. Such moments are common in dystopian fiction generally and have been a key feature of Eggers's work since the metafictional debates in *A Heartbreaking Work of Staggering Genius* and Will's lengthy internal monologues in *You Shall Know Our Velocity.* In *The Circle* these debates are designed to help the reader understand, and not merely experience, the protagonists' gradual conversion to the supposedly utopian ideology that governs the progress of one major technology company.

The story is set in an immediate future, one that bears much resemblance to the present. It follows the life of Mae Holland, a mostly sympathetic white middle-class girl in her mid-twenties. Mae grew up in Longfield, California, a small town of two thousand people near Fresno (9). After a few rebellious teenage years, she fled California for Carleton College, an expensive liberal arts school in southern Minnesota. Only twelve students in her graduating class attended a four-year college, and no one else traveled east of Colorado (9). After graduating with nearly a quarter of a million dollars of debt and few practical prospects or ambitions, Mae returned home to work for the local utility company, which was housed in a sickly green cinderblock office building.

In the early pages of the book, Eggers also introduces Annie, Mae's college roommate, who is on a very different trajectory. Annie is an energetic blond girl whose wealthy ancestors could be traced back to Plymouth Rock. While Mae was "meandering between majors, from art history to marketing to psychology," Annie graduated and finishes her MBA at Stanford (3). After school Annie became a top figure at the Circle, an Internet company that had revolutionized the world in less than six years (1). The company subsumed Google, Facebook, and Twitter by uniting Internet search and social media capabilities under one "Unified Operating System": "Anytime you wanted to see anything, use anything, comment on anything or buy anything, it was one button, one account, everything tied together and trackable and simple, all of it operable via mobile or laptop, tablet or retinal" (22).

The only caveat is that all users need to establish a TruYou, a single online identity, "unbendable and unmaskable" (21), that unites all facets of virtual existence. Despite scattered early protests about privacy and anonymity, the system swept the world and revolutionized the Internet. Comment boards became civil, "trolls" who deliberately disrupt online communications disappeared, and commerce became safe and easily trackable. The company rapidly expanded to control "90 percent of the search market. Eighty-eight percent of the free-mail market, 92 percent of text servicing" (174). Its dominant position in the market has brought in enormous amounts of money, which the company continually reinvests in cutting edge new ideas. It has promoted everything from reusable spacecrafts to tornado disruptors to a technology that, it is rumored, will replace "nighttime dreaming with organized thinking and real-life problem solving" (239).

The novel begins after Annie has gotten Mae a position at the Circle in the customer service department, which is euphemistically called "Customer Experience." In the opening pages, Mae arrives at the company's headquarters in California. The main offices are located on a sprawling four hundred–acre "campus" that provides a striking contrast to the operations of Mae's former employers, the anachronistic utility company that still uses punch cards and paper certificates of merit. The Circle attempts to meet all of its employees' needs, both personal and professional. As Mae's supervisor Dan explains during orientation, "we want this to be a workplace, sure, but it should also be a *human*place. . . . We're not automatons. This isn't a sweatshop. . . . This is a place where our humanity is respected, where our opinions are dignified, where our voices are heard—this is as important as any revenue, any stock price, any endeavor undertaken here" (47).

Services to meet nearly any need, from recreational activities to shopping to pet services, are provided for free on a campus littered with art and open green spaces. The buildings are dominated by glass and steel, and every surface seems meticulously planned, from Mae's organically shaped blond wood desk to the inspirational messages (DREAM, PARTICIPATE, FIND COMMUNITY, INNOVATE, IMAGINE, BREATHE) etched into stones on the pathways around campus. There are immaculately clean dorms with overstuffed couches and beds for employee use and a seemingly endless stream of entertainments offered around campus. One night Mae plans to stop by a poetry slam, a cooking class that will make use of an entire goat, a campaign against vaginal mutilation in Malawi, and a rag-tag collection of performers billed as the "Funk Arse Whole Circus" (163).

After her initial tour of campus, Mae can only gush: "outside the walls of the Circle, all was noise and struggle, failure and filth. But here, all had been perfected. The best people had made the best systems and the best systems had reaped funds, unlimited funds, that made possible this, the best place to work" (31). Mae is even allowed to include her father, who suffers from multiple sclerosis, on her insurance. When she seems reticent to ask, Annie chides her with one of the Circle's mantras: "Anything that makes our Circlers' lives better instantly becomes possible" (161). Most of the people Mae meets on campus are idealistic young employees, affectionately referred to as Circlers, who all seem to feel the same way—they flit around campus speaking about "world-changing" ideas and praising the new developments being sponsored by the company.

Mae's work, at least initially, seems rather mundane. She responds to questions and complaints from customers, generally doing little more than personalizing twenty stock replies to common issues. Customers are then given a survey and asked to rate Mae's performance from 1 to 100. Mae is encouraged to keep her aggregate score above 95 or so, which she does with little difficulty. New layers, however, are quickly added. Mae receives a participation score for engaging with social media. Her "PartiRank" shows how active she is in relation to other employees, though her orientation guide is quick to note, "it's just for fun. You're not judged by your rank or anything." She does quickly add, "Some Circlers take it very seriously, of course, and we love it when people participate" (102). Mae is also given a headset and asked to answer survey questions about products and preferences while she works. Both tasks are couched as opportunities for engagement, and her supervisors are reticent to describe them as obligations. When explaining the survey process, the project manager says, "Well, you have a certain, well, I don't want to say *quota*, but there's a number of questions that would be ideal and expected for you to answer in a given workday. Let's call it five hundred, but it might be more, might be less. . . . Most people can do five hundred in an hour, so it's not too stressful" (231).

Still, all of Mae's new obligations are explicitly monitored as part of her job. When she fails to respond to a fellow employee's invitation to a brunch for people who have been to Portugal, the "glitch" is written up, and Mae is cited for "non-participation in a classic sense" (109). She even gets a lecture for leaving campus too regularly. After visiting her sick father, her supervisor quickly acknowledges Mae's desire to spend time with her parents before complaining at length about Mae's lack of engagement in their community. "This isn't what you might call a clock in and clock out kind of company," he notes after another reprimand. "It's like we're driving you away" (176).

Initially Mae struggles to adjust to this merging of public and private spheres. She enjoys leaving campus to visit her parents in part because it allows her to disconnect for the weekend. She also goes kayaking alone on the bay to clear her head. One night she heads out to a distant island in the dark, a trip that would be strongly discouraged by the Coast Guard. In a moment typical for Eggers, she stops to marvel at the world, implicitly reveling in her own existence even as she acknowledges her obvious limitations. Facing the water and a nearby bridge humming with traffic, she is awed by the life all around her, both up above and hidden below the water. Yet "she didn't think too much about any of it. It was enough to be aware of the million permutations possible around her, and take comfort in knowing she would not, and really could not, know much at all" (272).

Despite such moments of peace, Mae is eager to succeed and rapidly adjusts to life in the Circle. She begins compulsively "zinging" her activities, and she stays up late into the night responding to online conversations. While the reader is primarily limited to Mae's viewpoint, and thus follows along with her gradual conversion, other characters emerge throughout the work as representatives of different ideological positions. In particular Mae's three love interests serve as rather blunt alternatives while she wrestles with her own place in this brave new world of technology.

Mercer is an old boyfriend who remains close with Mae's parents and helps out at their house, especially now that Mae's father has been having more trouble with his MS. Mercer dropped out of community college after two years and now has a successful local business making things out of antlers. He is an old-fashioned craftsman, and his primary function in the book is to vent about the evil influence of technology. He complains to Mae when she comes home, and, after they stop speaking because of Mae's increasing involvement with the Circle, he writes her several letters reiterating his concerns. First, he laments the emptiness of social media, which he likens to the nutritionless calories of fast food. Social media creates the illusion of activity but ultimately produces nothing. In a moment of exasperation, he attacks Mae for substituting virtual activity for real experience: "You look at pictures of Nepal, push a smile button, and you think that's the same as going there. I mean, what would happen if you actually went? Your CircleJerk ratings or whatever-the-fuck would drop below an acceptable level" (263).

Second, Mercer bemoans the impact that social media can have on consumers, who often become, according to Mercer, "socially autistic" in the real world. Moreover, these forms of engagement generate "unnaturally extreme social needs" as people feel compelled to superficially comment on everything and everyone they come across. (134). Finally, he argues that well-intentioned users place too much faith in those that control these technologies, willingly ceding control of their private lives in order to participate in the virtual social sphere. All of Mercer's fears are validated over the course of the book, and he ultimately flees north to avoid the ever-widening reach of the Circle. Between the company's expansion and Mae's gradual transformation, his symbolic death late in the novel seems preordained.

At the other extreme is Francis Garaventa, a young Circler whom Mae meets at the first party she attends. Francis is a socially awkward man with a tragic past. He spent most of his childhood bouncing around foster homes because his father was in prison and his mother was a drug addict. Two of his sisters, who were also moving through the system, were abducted and murdered. In the present Francis has fully embraced life at the Circle and is working to develop an implant that will make all children trackable. Initially his goal was to prevent abductions, but he is entirely unconcerned with privacy and readily agrees to have his worked utilized for an education program called YouthRank. The chip will be modified to transmit data not just about a child's location, but about his or her learning. The goal is to track "everything [a] student has learned. Every work they read, every word they looked up, every sentence they highlighted, every equation they wrote, every answer and correction. The guessswork of knowing where all students stand and what they know will be over" (345). This tracking will culminate in a global ranking of all students, so that each child will know precisely where they stand on a daily basis.

Francis's embrace of datafication and transparency initially causes friction with Mae, as when he secretly videotapes ones of their sexual encounters. To make matters worse, he refuses to delete the file because "technically neither one of us owns that video anymore. I couldn't delete it if I tried. It's like news. You don't own the news, even if it happens to you. You don't own history. It's part of the collective record now" (237–38). Functioning as a living confirmation of Mercer's theories, Francis, the embodiment of one aspect of the Circle's ideology, often struggles to communicate with Mae, and then, when the relationship progresses, he fails to engage even briefly in sexual activity with her. Despite his premature ejaculations, he insists, in typical Circle fashion, that Mae score the experience on a scale of 1–100.

Mae's final love interest is a mysterious figure named Kalden. She first meets him on her way to the bathroom. He is standing in the hall looking distracted. Kalden is the only person Mae encounters who seems dismissive of Circle culture, rolling his eyes and speaking flippantly about aspects of life on campus. Mae runs into him later at several parties, but he always prefers to linger at the edges, protected by shadows. The mystery deepens when Mae realizes that Kalden does not show up on any of the campus databases, nor does he appear on social media. As she becomes increasingly entangled in Circle culture, his secrecy drives her away, and, despite the friction with Francis, she often retreats to him in frustration. He is, after all, "utterly without mystery," always "available, familiar, locatable" (236–37). In contrast Kalden seems to represent the iconoclasm and unpredictability that the Circle's technology aims to mitigate and manage.

As the plot progresses, Kalden begins issuing vague warnings about the dangers of the Circle, but his position turns out to be quite distinct from Mercer's isolationism. Kalden has no objections to technology per se but feels that the company might fundamentally alter the balance between public and private. Society, he fears, is headed toward a place where all activity will be recorded and monitored by the Circle without allowing any opportunity for people to opt out. One company will control the flow of all information, paving the way for a "totalitarian nightmare" (486).

All three perspectives prove prescient as the novel progresses. The Circle continues to develop products that people want, but the scope of the employees' work expands with each major development. They create, for instance, a thumb-sized camera that can wirelessly transmit high-definition video from anywhere on the globe. It is "waterproof, sand-proof, wind-proof, animal-proof, insect-proof, everything-proof and costs only $59" (63–64). A product demonstration for Circle employees begins by showing the coastline; a few well-positioned cameras are great for checking surfing conditions. The vision, however, quickly expands from checking waves to experiencing life all over the globe to preventing human rights abuses. The presenter reveals live footage from Khartoum to Pyongyang, demonstrating the ease with which SeeChange cameras can be hidden despite the scrupulous watch of authoritarian regimes. He adds, "Tyrants can no longer hide. There needs to be, and will be, documentation and accountability, and we need to bear witness." The applause builds as the presentation reaches its dramatic conclusion, the logical endpoint of his line of thought: "To this end, I insist that all that happens should be known . . . we're losing the vast majority of what we do and see and learn. But it doesn't have to be that way. Not with these cameras, and not with the mission of the Circle" (68).

Having a world blanketed in cameras, with information constantly being uploaded to the cloud for processing, makes a whole host of other inventions possible. One proposal involves a security system that monitors all people and activity in a neighborhood. When someone who is not registered appears, everyone is notified. The explicit goal is to eliminate crime, but the cost is that everyone's movements will be recorded and monitored, at least electronically. As these ideas begin to coalesce, people at the Circle push for "total transparency." Mae volunteers as one of the first people to wear a camera around all the time. From the moment she wakes up until 10 P.M., with the exception of bathroom breaks, everything Mae does and sees is transmitted to the Internet. On her wrist she has a small screen that gives her instant access to viewer comments and tells her how many people are watching.

As might be expected, Mae initially struggles to adapt to her new life. If ideologically the cameras are supposed to provide an unvarnished look at the world, it quickly becomes apparent that they alter the reality in front of the lens. People must pretend to act naturally, and conversations alternate between being scripted and stilted. At an awkward dinner with her parents, Mae brings ingredients for dinner that must get screen time, and she is constantly worried that her parents will embarrass her on camera. Other people begin to distance themselves from Mae. Annie cuts off most contact with her, insisting that she is "too busy to have phone calls she could be proud of" (338). Mae also wears an earpiece, so that Additional Guidance can steer her around campus, ensuring that the audience will see particular products and innovations.

One other major effect of transparency is that Mae begins to modify her behavior. She starts with small changes, grabbing nuts instead of a brownie or being more conscious of her clothes. As the story progresses, she begins to experience a stronger pull: "Anything immoderate would provoke a flurry of zings of concern, so she stayed within the bounds of moderation. And she found it freeing. She was liberated from bad behavior. She was liberated from doing things she didn't want to be doing, eating and drinking things that did her no good" (331). Late in the story, Mae meets a man who had left divinity school to work with computers, and he pushes Mae's line of thinking even further. He says, "You're gonna save all the souls. . . . You're gonna teach them all the same things. There can be one morality, one set of rules. . . . Now we're all God. Every one of us will soon be able to see, and cast judgment upon, every other. We'll see what He sees. We'll articulate His judgment" (398). While the man is clearly drunk and Mae never explicitly endorses these ideas, he clearly echoes claims that Mae and other Circlers have made, with less explicit religious fervor, throughout the book. The Circle does, after all, inspire cultlike devotion in its young employees and promotes a clearly utopian ideology.

Moreover, as the novel progressions, mysterious references to "Completion" begin appearing around campus. Though the term is shrouded in mystery, it seems to reference the moment when every aspect of human existence will be saved and processed by the Circle. Employees are already living under constant observation or, for those more skeptical of the process, supervision.

As part of the health care program, they have ingested organic sensors that monitor every aspect of their bodily functions, from the pH balance of their sweat to their sleep patterns. Soon, TruYouth, the name for their educational scanners, will track everything a person reads or learns. The Circle also begins a massive campaign to digitize every photo, every newsreel, every amateur video, and every bit of available security footage to create as complete a record of the past as is possible.

Though there are brief mentions throughout the early pages about regulatory difficulties and privacy concerns, the movement toward completion brings the political dimensions of the work into sharper focus. Just months after the first politician pledges to "go clear," it becomes nearly mandatory for any aspiring officeholder to do the same. The novel does not interrogate the issues involved too closely. Eggers never, for instance, seriously engages with questions about national security. He instead emphasizes the complex interconnections between corporations and government as well as the ways in which seemingly good impulses (we should be aware of what our elected officials are doing!) can lead to unintended consequences. When someone suggests that the government could save hundreds of billions of dollars by holding elections through TruYou accounts, Mae raises the possibility of mandatory Circle accounts. Why stop at private commerce when all government activity could also be run more efficiently through the Circle? Again good intentions mask the underlying perils of such a system, and Mercer's ominous words hang over the latter pages of the text: "do not presume the benevolence of your leaders" (261).

In the case of the Circle, there are, again symbolically, three different leaders. The first is Ty Gospodinov, the reclusive young visionary who developed the Unified Operating System. He is rarely seen, except for the occasional video feed at a campus event. Eamon Bailey is the face of the company, an avuncular figure with a poetic sensibility who wants to harness the technology of the Circle to capture every facet of life on Earth. It is his dream to make all people their best selves through constant surveillance, and he openly promotes mantras such as "privacy is theft" and "secrets are lies." Finally, there is Tom Stenton, the capitalist who monetizes all of these ideas and makes the expansion of the Circle possible. Stenton, an ostentatious capitalist, gives weight to Mercer's concerns in the last pages of the book. Eamon espouses an extreme philosophy but seems to genuinely care about people. Ty is motivated by curiosity and a desire to make the Internet experience more "civil." Tom seems motivated primarily by power and money, and so he represents the greatest threat to the utopian dream of the Circle community.

In an obviously symbolic moment at the end of the book, the three Wise Men, as the leaders are called by the Circle community, gather to see three new creatures captured from deep within the Marianas Trench (in a submersible designed at the Circle, of course). There is a male sea horse, the symbolic corollary to Ty, who hides while his babies float aimlessly in a group above (the Circlers). There is a shape-shifting octopus (Eamon Bailey) who is constantly exploring with his tentacles, as if he wants to know about every inch of the tank. Finally, there is a voracious shark (Tom) who seems able to consume nearly anything. Early in the novel, they feed the shark a sea turtle, and it digests its pray, shell and all, in a matter of seconds. At the close of the novel, the Wise Men put all three creatures, ostensibly from the same habitat, together in a beautiful aquarium. They feed the shark all day and place large tuna in the tank to distract him, but these safety measures prove inadequate. The shark consumes the tuna, then eats the octopus and all the seahorses, before finally turning its attention to the coral and seaweed within the tank. He eats until there is nothing left.

The end of the story turns on this rather predictable struggle. Ty, who turns out to be Mae's mysterious lover Kalden, is a true artist/visionary. He plans to dismantle the Circle and thwart Tom, but, for reasons that are not entirely clear, he needs Mae's help. (He repeatedly references Mae's visibility and her importance to the Circle.) Over the course of the book, Mae has progressed from a sympathetic woman who resists intrusions on her privacy by unplugging and kayaking to someone who retreats from her problems by answering customer queries and scanning social media. Her choice seems inevitable. As Ty unveils his counter-strategies, Mae equates him with Mercer, a paranoid lunatic who cannot understand how close the Circle is to achieving social perfection. In the closing pages, Mae remains loyal to the company and reveals Ty's plans to his partners. The novel ends with Mae in a hospital, watching over Annie, who has had a nervous breakdown after the Circle's data-mining publicly unearthed chilling information about her parents. Mae is angry that she has no access to comatose Annie's thoughts and plans to bring it up at the next meeting.

While the ending reduces, for the sake of narrative, rather complicated issues into a struggle between an all-consuming capitalist shark and an independent visionary, the book as a whole is far more interested in the social and psychological effects of contemporary technology than in pointing fingers. Nearly all of the technological developments imagined in the book are meant to serve positive ends, a cast that gives Eggers's probing of the thin line between choice and coercion in contemporary consumer society more force. The concept of "choice" becomes even more difficult given the impatience bred by technologies that encourage immediate response and offer instantaneous access to nearly any information. Each time a new product is unveiled, people clamor for it immediately without ever stopping to reflect on its broader implications.

The novel also underscores the way in which supposedly "transparent" media alter reality and generate a new performative mode of behavior, one that further encourages action over reflection. When the Circle tests its new voting platform, the engineers ask a series of sample questions, which the employees answer quickly. One question, however, attempts to simulate a national security emergency. A terrorist leader has supposedly been found, and the president wants to know whether or not the American people would approve of the collateral damage necessitated by a drone strike. Mae is pleased to see the Circlers taking their responsibility seriously, as they consider the question for almost a whole minute. After seventy-one seconds, all responses are tallied. With very little information and no knowledge of who was providing it, 71 percent of Circlers have favored the drone strike.

Such near-immediate communication also encourages, as Mercer warns, a certain kind of neediness and social relations dominated by "pre-emptive validation" (390). Mae, for instance, always gives Francis a score of 100 for his sexual performance, even when they do not manage to engage in sex. She also becomes distraught after the voting system jokingly asks, "Is Mae Holland awesome or what?" Though 97 percent of the campus "smiles," she fixates on the handful of people who "frowned" at her. She imagines them hating her, then wanting to kill her, and finally wishing she had never been born. Mae finds peace only when she resolves to win each person over, one by one.

Given the focus of the book, it reads more like a parable than a nuanced exploration of alternative futures, and Eggers seems more interested in outlining implications and offering warnings than providing solutions. At most, *The Circle* advocates for "balance" and a more thoughtful approach to the implementation of technology, while still acknowledging the impulses that drive people, often times for very good reasons, to press for immediate change. Eggers also reminds us that these changes are never completely innocent. Those figures who control the flow of information or make alternatives visible always shape the outcome. And even the most utopian projects are still underscored by various forms of self-interest. Mae embraces the Circle in part because it helps her make sense of her chaotic existence, and she often bemoans the lack of more, not less, help in making her decisions. Late in the book, the narrator notes, "the elegance of it all, the ideological purity of the Circle, of real transparency, gave her peace, a warming feeling of logic and order" (419).

As new technologies reshape privacy and individuality, Mae loses the close personal relationships that she has early on in the text and gives up her quiet reflections for the constant, but perhaps less meaningful, validation available on social media. At its best *The Circle* acknowledges the complex psychological and social forces underscoring these changes and explores the difference between transparency and surveillance, protection and imprisonment, and visibility and accountability in an increasingly connected world. It also provides an interesting perspective on many of Eggers's earlier preoccupations. The "lattice" from *A.H.W.O.S.G.*, for instance, takes on a far different meaning in the virtual age than it did in the time of the *Real World*. Other crucial elements of Eggers's earlier perspective, however, remain intact, if only through their absence in the emerging totalitarian world of the Circle. While this novel ultimately shies away from adopting a purely journalistic perspective, it nonetheless magnifies elements of contemporary culture to provide a provocative look at some of the dangers and possibilities emerging from the quest for technological "progress."

NOTES

Chapter 1: Understanding Dave Eggers

1. Anushka Asthana, "The 100 Best Books of the Decade," *Times* (London), accessed November 14, 2012, http://entertainment.timesonline.co.uk/tol/arts_and_entertainment/books/book_reviews/article6914181.ece?print=yes&randnum=1258482707214.

2. Keith Goetzman et al., "50 Visionaries Who Are Changing Your World," *Utne Reader,* accessed August 1, 2013, http://www.utne.com/2008-11-13/50-visionaries-who-are-changing-your-world.aspx#axzz2wNTV5ImA.

3. For a few references to the controversy, see Keith Gessen, "Keith Gessen on Dave Eggers," *Crime City USA,* November 13, 2012, accessed August 1, 2013, http://crimecityusa.blogspot.com; Amy Harmon, "Amazon Glitch Unmasks War of Reviewers," *New York Times,* February 14, 2004, accessed August 1, 2013, http://www.nytimes.com/2004/02/14/technology/14AMAZ.html; and Johannes Lichtman, "I've Been Enlisted by Dave Eggers and the McSweeney's Crew for a Super Secret Conspiracy," *Bling Theory: A Blog about Books and Bling. But mostly Books,* January 1, 2013, accessed August 1, 2013, http://www.blingtheory.net/post/39959989027/ive-been-enlisted-by-dave-eggers-and-the-mcsweeneys.

4. Gary Krist, "The Lost Boy," *Washington Post,* accessed August 1, 2013, http://www.washingtonpost.com/wp-dyn/content/article/2006/12/15/AR2006121501451.html.

5. Lee Siegel, "The Niceness Racket," *New Republic* 236, no. 14 (2007): 53.

6. Ibid., 50.

7. Sarah Brouillette, "Paratextuality and Economic Disavowal in Dave Eggers' *You Shall Know Our Velocity,*" *Reconstruction: Studies in Contemporary Culture* 3, no. 2 (2003): 1.

8. "Diary of a Media Hoax: The Death of Adam Rich," *AlterNet,* April 25, 2000, accessed August 1, 2013, www.alternet.org/story/7572/diary_of_a_media_hoax%3A_the_death_of_adam_rich.

9. Saadi Soudavar, "An Interview with Dave Eggers," *Harvard Advocate Online,* Summer 2000, accessed August 1, 2013, http://www.armchairnews.com/freelance/eggers.html.

10. Daisy Maryles, "Behind the Bestsellers," *Publishers Weekly* 247, no. 16 (2000): 21.

11. Kim Curtis, "Searching for the Real Dave Eggers," *Star Banner* [Ocala, Fla.], April 29, 2001, D3.

12. Jonathan D'Amore, *American Authorship and Autobiographical Narrative: Mailer, Wideman, Eggers* (New York: Palgrave, 2012), 178.

13. Duncan Campbell, "What Do They Mean?," *Guardian*, September 22, 2003, G2: 6.

14. "*L.A. Times* Announces 2009 Book Prize Finalists," *Los Angeles Times* blog, "Jacket Copy: Books, Authors and All Things Bookish," *Los Angeles Times*, February 22, 2010, accessed August 1, 2013, http://latimesblogs.latimes.com/jacketcopy/2010/02/latimes-book-prizes-2009.html.

Chapter 2: *A Hearbreaking Work of Staggering Genius*

1. Dave Eggers, *A Heartbreaking Work of Staggering Genius* (New York: Vintage, 2001). Subsequent citations appear as page numbers in the text.

2. The book was first published on February 17, 2000, and remained on the *New York Times* best-seller list until June, peaking at number 4 in late March.

3. Sara Mosle, "My Brother's Keeper," *New York Times Book Review* 149, no. 51304 (2000): 6.

4. Elise Harris, "Infinite Jest," *Nation* 270, no. 11 (2000): 46.

5. "Paratexts" is Gerard Genette's term for the "accompanying productions" of a literary work (1). In Genette's taxonomy, paratexts can include both materials physically connected with a work (introductory and concluding sections) and those circulated separately (marketing materials). See Gerard Genette, *Paratexts: Thresholds of Interpretation*, trans. Jane E. Lewin (New York: Cambridge University Press, 1997).

6. Mark Horowitz, "Laughing through His Tearjerker," *New York* 33, no. 4 (January 2000): 33.

7. Michiko Kakutani, "Clever Young Man Raises Sweet Little Brother," *New York Times*, February 1, 2000, E8.

8. Lee Siegel, "The Niceness Racket," *New Republic* 236, no. 14 (2007): 50.

9. Ibid.

Chapter 3: *You Shall Know Our Velocity*

1. Dave Eggers, *You Shall Know Our Velocity* (San Francisco: McSweeney's, 2002). Subsequent citations appear as page numbers in the text.

2. Aliki Varvogli, *Travel and Dislocation in Contemporary American Fiction* (New York: Routledge, 2012), 53.

3. Wen Stephenson, "Re: No Subject," *Agni* 58 (2003): 205.

4. Caren Irr, "Toward the World Novel: Genre Shifts in Twenty-First-Century Expatriate Fiction," *American Literary History* 23, no. 3 (2011): 666.

5. Peter Kurth, "'You Shall Know Our Velocity' by Dave Eggers," *Salon Media Group*, October 31, 2002, http://www.salon.com/2002/10/31/eggers_3/. Accessed August 1, 2013.

6. Irr, "Toward the World Novel," 665.

Chapter 4: *What Is the What*

1. Dave Eggers, *What Is the What: The Autobiography of Valentino Achak Deng: A Novel* (New York: Vintage, 2007). Subsequent citations appear as page numbers in the text.

2. Thomas Jones, "This Is Not That Place," *London Review of Books* 29, no. 12 (June 2007): 24.

3. Dave Eggers, "It Was Just Boys Walking," *Guardian Review*, May 25, 2007, 4.

4. Dave Eggers and Valentino Achak Deng, "Interview with Dave Eggers and Valentino Achak Deng," *VAD: The Valentino Achak Deng Foundation,* n.p., May 2013, accessed August 1, 2013, http://www.valentinoachakdeng.org/interview.php.

5. Aliki Varvogli, *Travel and Dislocation in Contemporary American Fiction* (New York: Routledge, 2012), 24.

6. "Fictionalized AB in Valentino's voice." "Interview with Dave Eggers and Valentino Achak Deng." *VAD: The Valention Achak Deng Foundation.* http://www.vadfoundation.org/interview.php. Accessed August 1, 2013.

7. Kevin Brooks, "Dave Eggers's 'What Is the What' as World Literature," *World Literature Today* (March–April 2010): 40.

8. Lee Siegel, "The Niceness Racket," *New Republic* 236, no. 14 (2007): 31.

9. Ibid., 27.

Chapter 5: *Zeitoun*

1. Dave Eggers, *Zeitoun* (New York: Vintage, 2010). Subsequent citations appear as page numbers in the text.

2. Victoria Patterson, "Did Dave Eggers Get 'Zeitoun' Wrong?," *Salon Media Group,* December 9, 2012, accessed August 1, 2013, http://www.salon.com/2012/12/09/did_dave_egers_get_zeitoun_wrong/.

3. Sarah Foss, "Trying to Read 'Zeitoun,'" *Foss Forward: A Daily Gazette Life Blog,* December 10, 2012, http://www.dailygazette.com/weblogs/foss/2012/dec/10/trying-read-zeitoun/.

4. Edward Champion, "Dave Eggers, National Book Award Finalist, Refuses to Answer about Abdulrahman Zeitoun's Violent Assaults," *Reluctant Habits,* November 14, 2012, accessed August 1, 2013, http://www.edrants.com/dave-eggers-national-book-award-finalist-refuses-to-answer-about-abjulrahman-zeitouns-violent-assaults/.

5. Adam Martin, "Zeitoun, Dave Eggers' Post-Katrina Hero, Faces Murder Solicitation Charges," *The Atlantic Wire,* August 9, 2012, accessed August 1, 2013, www.theatlanticwire.com/national/2012/08/zeitoun-dave-eggers-post-katrina-hero-faces-murder-solicitation-charges/55618/.

6. Anis Shivani, "An Interview with Dave Eggers about *Zeitoun,*" *Colorado Review* 37, no. 2 (Summer 2010): 59.

7. Lee Siegel, "The Niceness Racket," *New Republic* 236, no. 14 (2007): 50.

Chapter 6: Short Stories, Short Short Stories, and Films

1. Dave Eggers, *How We Are Hungry* (New York: Vintage, 2004). Subsequent citations appear as page numbers in the text.

2. Joanna Briscoe, "Short Cuts to the Real Thing," *Guardian Review,* March 25, 2005, 27.

3. This is not to say that Eggers's more recent texts are not formally inventive. He does not, however, explicitly draw attention to formal elements quite as regularly in his later texts.

4. Dave Eggers, "Short and Sweet," *Guardian,* June 18, 2004, http://www.theguardian.com/books/2004/jun/18/shortshortstories.fiction.

5. Dave Eggers, *How Water Feels to the Fishes* (San Francisco: McSweeney's, 2007), 20. Subsequent citations appear as page numbers in the text.

6. "Box Office/Business for *Where the Wild Things Are,*" *Internet Movie Database,* accessed on August 1, 2013, http://www.imdb.com/title/tt0386117/business?ref_=tt_ql_dt_4.

7. A. O. Scott, "Practicing Virtue, and Proud of It," *New York Times,* June 5, 2009, C1.

8. Stephanie Zacharek, "*Away We Go,*" *Salon Media Group,* June 5, 2009, http://www.salon.com/2009/06/05/away_we_go/.

9. Dave Eggers, *The Wild Things* (San Francisco: McSweeney's, 2009). Subsequent citations appear as page numbers in the text.

Chapter 7: A Hologram for the King

1. Dave Eggers, *A Hologram for the King* (San Francisco: McSweeney's, 2012), 20. Subsequent citations appear as page numbers in the text.

2. Samuel Beckett, *Waiting for Godot* (New York: Grove Press, 1954), 51.

Afterword

1. Dave Eggers, *The Circle* (New York: Vintage, 2014). Subsequent citations appear as page numbers in the text.

2. *The Circle* was published in October 2013, shortly after the manuscript for *Understanding Dave Eggers* was completed. If a chapter was added every time Eggers completed a new project, this work would remain "in progress" for the foreseeable future. At the same time, *The Circle* has received considerable attention and this text would be incomplete without some mention of it. This afterword provides a brief survey of the work that is informed by the previous analyses.

SELECTED BIBLIOGRAPHY

Works by Dave Eggers

NOVELS

The Circle. New York: Vintage, 2014.

A Hologram for the King. San Francisco: McSweeney's, 2012.

Sacrament: Hand's Revised Edition. San Francisco: McSweeney's, 2003.

The Unforbidden Is Compulsory; or, Optimism. San Francisco: McSweeney's, 2004.

What Is the What: The Autobiography of Valentino Achak Deng: A Novel. New York: McSweeney's, 2006.

The Wild Things. San Francisco: McSweeney's, 2009.

You Shall Know Our Velocity. San Francisco: McSweeney's, 2002.

You Shall Know Our Velocity! New York: Vintage, 2003.

COLLECTIONS

How the Water Feels to the Fishes. San Francisco: McSweeney's, 2007.

How We Are Hungry. New York: Vintage, 2004.

It Is Right to Draw Their Fur: Animal Renderings by Dave Eggers. San Francisco: McSweeney's, 2010.

Short Short Stories. London and New York: Penguin, 2005.

As Lucy Thomas. *Jokes Told in Heaven about Babies*. San Francisco: McSweeney's, 2003.

MEMOIRS

A Heartbreaking Work of Staggering Genius. New York: Simon & Schuster, 2000.

"Mistakes We Knew We Were Making." *A Heartbreaking Work of Staggering Genius*. New York: Vintage, 2001. 1–41.

SELECT NONFICTION

"Diary of a Media Hoax: The Death of Adam Rich." *AlterNet.org*, April 25, 2000. Accessed August 1, 2013. www.alternet.org/story/7572/diary_of_a_media_hoax%3A_the_death_of_adam_rich. Accessed August 1, 2013.

"It Was Just Boys Walking." *Guardian Review*, May 25, 2007, 4.

"Short and Sweet." *Theguardian.com*, June 18, 2004. Accessed August 1, 2013. http://www.theguardian.com/books/2004/jun/18/shortshortstories.fiction.

Zeitoun. New York: McSweeney's, 2006.

Eggers, Dave, Daniel Moulthrop, and Nínive Clements Calegari. *Teachers Have It Easy: The Big Sacrifices and Small Salaries of America's Teachers*. New York: New Press, 2005.

Eggers, Dave, and Valentino Achak Deng. "Interview with Dave Eggers and Valentino Achak Deng." *VAD: The Valentino Achak Deng Foundation,* May 2013. Accessed August 1, 2013. http://www.valentinoachakdeng.org/interview.php.

Secondary Sources

826 National. "About 826 National." Accessed August 1, 2013. http://www.i26national.org/about/.

Altes, Liesbeth Korthals. "Sincerity, Reliability and Other Ironies—Notes on Dave Eggers' *A Heartbreaking Work of Staggering Genius.*" In *Narrative Unreliability in the Twentieth- Century First-Person Novel,* edited by Elke D'hoker and Gunther Martens. Berlin and New York: Walter de Gruyter, 2008.

Ashtor, Gila G. "Erotic Mourning and Post-traumatic Sexual Desire." *CLCWeb: Comparative Literature and Culture* 12, no. 3 (2010). Accessed August 1, 2013. http://dx.doi.org/10.7771/1481-4378.1543.

Asthana, Anushka. "The 100 Best Books of the Decade." *The Times* (London), November 14, 2009. Accessed August 1, 2013. http://entertainment.timesonline.co.uk/tol/arts_and_entertainment/books/book_reviews/article6914181.ece?print=yes&randnum=1258482707214.

Atwood, Margaret. "When Privacy Is Theft." *New York Times Review of Books.* November 21, 2013. Accessed May 18, 2014. http://www.nybooks.com/articles/archives/2013/nov/21/eggers-circle-when-privacy-is-theft.

Beckett, Samuel. *Waiting for Godot.* New York: Grove Press, 1954.

Bennett, Laura. "5 Things Dave Eggers Fundamentally Misunderstands about the Internet." *New Republic.* October 15, 2013. Accessed on May 18, 2014. http://www.newrepublic.com/article/115203/5-things-dave-eggers-fundamentally-misunderstands-about-Internet.

Bone, Martyn. "Narratives of African Immigration to the U.S. South: Dave Eggers's *What Is the What* and Cynthia Shearer's *The Celestial Jukebox.*" *CR: The New Centennial Review* 10, no. 1 (2010): 65–76.

Briscoe, Joanna. "Short Cuts to the Real Thing." *Guardian Review,* March 25, 2005, 27.

Brooks, Kevin. "Dave Eggers's 'What Is the What' as World Literature." *World Literature Today* 84, no. 2 (March–April 2010): 36–40.

Brouillette, Sarah. "Paratextuality and Economic Disavowal in Dave Eggers' *You Shall Know Our Velocity.*" *Reconstruction: Studies in Contemporary Culture* 3, no. 2 (Spring 2003): 1–26.

Campbell, Duncan. "What Do They Mean?" *Guardian,* September 22, 2003, sec. G2: 6.

Champion, Edward. "Dave Eggers, National Book Award Finalist, Refuses to Answer about Abdulrahman Zeitoun's Violent Assaults." *Reluctant Habits* blog, November 14, 2012. Accessed August 1, 2013. http://www.edrants.com/dave-eggers-national-book-award-finalist-refuses-to-answer-about-abjulrahman-zeitouns-violent-assaults/.

Corliss, Richard. "*Away We Go:* We're OK, You're All Idiots." *Time.com,* June 6, 2009. Accessed August 1, 2013. http://content.time.com/time/arts/article/0,0599,1903238,00.html.

Curtis, Kim. "Searching for the Real Dave Eggers." *Star Banner* [Ocala, Fla.], April 29, 2001, sec. D: 3.

D'Amore, Jonathan. *American Authorship and Autobiographical Narrative: Mailer, Wideman, Eggers*. New York: Palgrave, 2012.

Eaglestone, Robert. "'You Would Not Add to My Suffering if You Knew What I Have Seen': Holocaust Testimony and Contemporary African Trauma Literature." *Studies in the Novel* 40, no. 1–2 (Spring–Summer 2008): 72–85.

Foss, Sara. "Trying to Read 'Zeitoun.'" *Dailygazette.com*. Foss Forward: A *Daily Gazette* Life blog, December 10, 2012. Accessed August 1, 2013. http://www.dailygazette.com/weblogs/foss/2012/dec/10/trying-read-zeitoun/.

Funk, Wolfgang. "The Quest for Authenticity: Dave Eggers's *A Heartbreaking Work of Staggering Genius* between Fiction and Reality." In *The Metareferential Turn in Contemporary Arts and Media: Forms, Functions, Attempts at Explanation*, edited by Werner Wolf, 125–44. Amsterdam and New York: Rodpi, 2011.

Genette, Gerard. *Paratexts: Thresholds of Interpretation*. Translated by Jane E. Lewin. New York: Cambridge University Press, 1997.

Gessen, Keith. "Keith Gessen on Dave Eggers." *Crime City USA* blog, November 13, 2012. Accessed August 1, 2013. http://crimecityusa.blogspot.com.

Goetzman, Keith, Julie Hanus, Judith Lewis, Hannah Lobel, Danielle Maestretti, and Elizabeth Ryan. "50 Visionaries Who Are Changing Your World." *Utne.com*. Utne Reader. Accessed August 1, 2013. http://www.utne.com/2008-11-13/50-visionaries-who-are-changing-your-world.aspx#axzz2wNTV5ImA.

Gutierrez, Claire. "Behind the Cover Story: Dave Eggers on Imagining the Future World of Over-Sharing." *New York Times Magazine*. Accessed on May 18, 2014. http://6thfloor.blogs.nytimes.com/2013/09/28/behind-the-cover-story-dave-eggers-on-imagining-the-future-world-of-over-sharing./

Hamilton, Caroline. "Blank Looks: Reality TV and Memoir in *A Heartbreaking Work of Staggering Genius*." *Australasian Journal of American Studies* 28, no. 2 (December 2009): 31–46.

———. *One Man Zeitgeist: Dave Eggers, Publishing and Publicity*. London and New York: Bloomsbury Academic, 2012.

Harmon, Amy. "Amazon Glitch Unmasks War of Reviewers." *New York Times*, February 14, 2004. Accessed August 1, 2013. http://www.nytimes.com/2004/02/14/technology/14AMAZ.html.

Harris, Elise. "Infinite Jest." *Nation* 270, no. 11 (2000): 45–48.

Horowitz, Mark. "Laughing through His Tearjerker." *New York* 33, no. 4 (January 2000): 30–33.

Huehls, Mitchum. "Referring to the Human in Contemporary Human Rights Literature." *MFS: Modern Fiction Studies* 58, no. 1 (Spring 2012): 1–21.

"Illini Union One Book, One Campus." University of Illinois at Urbana. Accessed August 1, 2013. http://www.illinois.edu/pa/one_book_one_campus.html.

Internet Movie Database. "Box Office/Business for *Where the Wild Things Are*." n.d.Accessed August 1, 2013. http://www.imdb.com/title/tt0386117/business?ref_=tt_ql_dt_4.

Irr, Caren. "Toward the World Novel: Genre Shifts in Twenty-First-Century Expatriate Fiction." *American Literary History* 23, no. 3 (2011): 660–79.

Jones, Thomas. "This Is Not That Place." *London Review of Books* 29, no. 12 (June 2007): 23–24.

Kakutani, Michiko. "Clever Young Man Raises Sweet Little Brother." *New York Times,* February 1, 2000, E8.

Krist, Gary. "The Lost Boy." *Washington Post,* December 17, 2006. Accessed August 1, 2013. http://www.washingtonpost.com/wp-dyn/content/article/2006/12/15/AR2006121501451.html.

Kurth, Peter. "'You Shall Know Our Velocity' by Dave Eggers." *Salon Media Group,* October 31, 2002. Accessed August 1, 2013. http://www.salon.com/2002/10/31/eggers_3/.

"*L.A. Times* Announces 2009 Book Prize finalists." *Los Angeles Times* blog, February 22, 2010. Accessed August 1, 2013. http://latimesblogs.latimes.com/jacketcopy/2010/02/latimes-book-prizes-2009.html.

Lichtman, Johannes. "I've Been Enlisted by Dave Eggers and the McSweeney's Crew for a Super Secret Conspiracy." Bling Theory: A Blog about Books and Bling. But Mostly Books, January 1, 2013. Accessed August 1, 2013. http://www.blingtheory.net/post/39959989027/ive-been-enlisted-by-dave-eggers-and-the-mcsweeneys.

Martin, Adam. "Zeitoun, Dave Eggers' Post-Katrina Hero, Faces Murder Solicitation Charges." *The Atlantic Wire,* August 9, 2012. Accessed August 1, 2013. www.theatlanticwire.com/national/2012/08/zeitoun-dave-eggers-post-katrina-hero-faces-murder-solicitation-charges/55618/.

Maryles, Daisy. "Behind the Bestsellers." *Publishers Weekly* 247, no. 16 (2000): 21.

McSweeney's. "About." *Wholphin.* http://store.mcsweeneys.net/t/categories/wholphin/about/. Accessed August 1, 2013.

McSweeney's. "About the *Believer.*" *Believer.* Accessed August 1, 2013. http://www.believermag.com/about/.

McSweeney's. "A Brief Q&A with Dave Eggers About His New Novel, *The Circle.*" *Timothy McSweeney's Internet Tendency.* Accessed on May 18, 2014. http://www.mcsweeneys.net/articles/a-brief-q-a-with-dave-eggers-about-his-new-novel-the-circle.

Mosle, Sara. "My Brother's Keeper." *New York Times Book Review* 149, no. 51304 (February 2000): 6.

Patterson, Victoria. "Did Dave Eggers Get 'Zeitoun' Wrong?" *Salon Media Group,* December 9, 2012. Accessed August 1, 2013. http://www.salon.com/2012/12/09/did_dave_eggers_get_zeitoun_wrong/.

Peek, Michelle. "Humanitarian Narrative and Posthumanist Critique: Dave Eggers's *What Is the What.*" *Biography* 35, no. 1 (Winter 2012): 115–36.

Powell, Katrina M. "Rhetorics of Displacement: Constructing Identities in Forced Relocations." *College English* 74, no. 4 (March 2012): 299–324.

Salmon, Felix. "How Dave Eggers Gets Silicon Valley Wrong." *Reuters.* Accessed on May 18, 2014. http://blogs.reuters.com/felix-salmon/2013/09/30/how-dave-eggers-gets-silicon-valley-wrong.

Samples, Suzanne R. "Interrupting the Puppet Master: (Un)reliability and Metatextaulity in Dave Eggers's *You Shall Know Our Velocity.*" Master's thesis, Marshall University, 2007.

Scott, A. O. "Practicing Virtue, and Proud of It." *New York Times,* June 5, 2009, sec. C: 1.

Shivani, Anis. "An Interview with Dave Eggers about *Zeitoun.*" *Colorado Review* 37, no. 2 (Summer 2010): 56–67.

Siegel, Lee. "The Niceness Racket." *New Republic* 236, no. 14 (2007): 49–53.

Smith, Sidonie, and Julia Watson. "The Rumpled Bed of Autobiography." *Biography* 24, no. 1 (2001): 1–14.

Soudavar, Saadi. "An Interview with Dave Eggers." *Harvard Advocate Online,* Summer 2000. Accessed August 1, 2013. http://www.armchairnews.com/freelance/eggers.html.

Stam, Robert. *Literature through Film: Realism, Magic, and the Art of Adaptation.* Malden, MA: Blackwell, 2005.

Stephenson, Wen. "Re: No Subject." *Agni* 58 (2003): 202–21.

Thomas, Valorie. "'Dust To Cleanse Themselves,' A Survivor's Ethos: Diasporic Disidentifications in *Zeitoun.*" *Biography* 35, no. 2 (Spring 2012): 271–85.

Twitchell, Elizabeth. "Dave Eggers's *What Is the What:* Fictionalizing Trauma in the Era of Misery Lit." *American Literature* 83, no. 3 (September 2011): 621–48.

Varvogli, Aliki. *Travel and Dislocation in Contemporary American Fiction.* New York: Routledge, 2012.

Widiss, Benjamin. *Obscure Invitations: The Persistence of the Author in Twentieth-Century American Literature.* Stanford: Stanford University Press, 2011.

Winter, Jessica. "All That Happens Must Be Known." *Slate.com.* October 3, 2013. Accessed May 18, 2014. http://www.slate.com/articles/technology/books/2013/10/dave_eggers_tech_novel_the_circle_reviewed.html.

Yost, Brian. "The Voices of Others: Dave Eggers and New Directions for Testimony Narrative and Cosmopolitan Literary Collaboration." *Ariel: A Review of International English Literature* 42, no. 1 (2011): 149–70.

Zacharek, Stephanie. "*Away We Go.*" *Salon Media Group,* June 5, 2009. Accessed August 1, 2013. http://www.salon.com/2009/06/05/away_we_go/.

INDEX

ABOUT THE AUTHOR

TIMOTHY W. GALOW is an assistant professor of English at Carroll University in Waukesha, Wisconsin. He has published widely on American literature, modern celebrity culture, film, and contemporary rhetoric. Galow's most recent work is *Writing Celebrity: Stein, Fitzgerald, and the Modern(ist) Art of Self-Fashioning*.